GLUTEN FREE VEGETARIAN MEDITERRANEAN RECIPES

Sanaa Abourezk

GLUTEN FREE VEGETARIAN MEDITERRANEAN RECIPES

Sanaa Abourezk

PALMYRA
PUBLISHING

To my dad.

I'll love you forever.

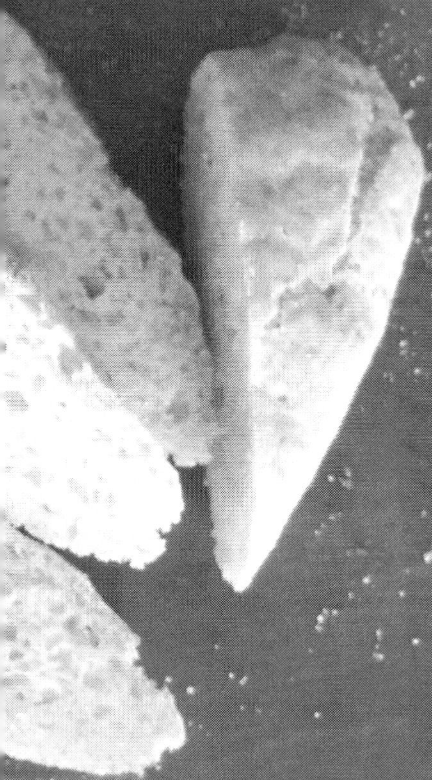

TABLE OF CONTENTS

SALADS

MAIN DISHES

SAVORY BAKING

SWEET BAKING

INTRODUCTION

If you're buying this book, you already know the details of Celiac Disease and Gluten Sensitivity, so I will spare you the redundant details and statistics.

I believe that most allergies from which we suffer are due to the processed food to which our families are exposed. Reading the list ingredients on any package of food is much like taking a course in chemistry and in foreign language.

If you are serious about escaping food allergies and pursuing healthy eating you need only to spend more time in your kitchen cooking from scratch rather than spending time in the aisles of supermarkets, or watching cooking shows on television while eating a frozen dinner.

Since I published my first gluten free book, I challenged myself to create recipes that everyone in the family can enjoy, whether or not they are sensitive to gluten. I'm blessed with customers in my restaurant who are willing to render their opinions about the new dishes I create and set down in front of them.

The recipes are simple, easy to make, and will entice you back to the kitchen to once again cook what can be healthy and tasty food. As you can tell from the title, the food in this book is based on Mediterranean cuisine, from the Eastern Mediterranean, to Southern Europe, and North Africa.

You will see a lot of recipes calling for cooked rice, which in the absence of wheat gluten, becomes the glue that holds together the other ingredients.

Also you will find that I had two combinations of flour for this book, gluten free flour that is for savory baking, and gluten free flour for sweet baking.

I've found that to avoid the mess created by using different kinds of flour each time you cook one of these recipes, I mix all the flours used for savory cooking in one large container, with a tightly closed lid. I do the same for sweet flours.

You may like different combinations of gluten free flours, but I've found that the ones included in this cookbook work the best for me.

I hope that you will dive into this cookbook, enjoy the recipes and the food derived from the recipes. And feel free to contact me with any questions or suggestions you may have.

Happy cooking,
Sanaa Abourezk

APPETIZERS

Eggplant Caviar
Serves 4-6

2	one-pound eggplants
3	cloves garlic, mashed
½	cup chopped parsley
3	tablespoons olive oil
3	tablespoons lemon juice

salt to taste

With a fork, punch a couple of holes in each eggplant. Broil or grill the eggplant until the skin is charred.

Cool and then peel the skin. Mash the eggplant into a smooth paste.

Add the rest of the ingredients. Refrigerate for a couple of hours before serving.

Baba Ghanouj
Serves 4-6

2   **one-pound eggplants**
3   **cloves garlic, mashed**
4   **tablespoons tahini**
1   **cup plain yogurt**
½   **teaspoon cumin**
salt to taste

With a fork, punch a couple of holes in the eggplants. Broil or grill the eggplant until the skin is charred.

Cool. Peel the skin and mash the eggplant.

Mix in the rest of the ingredients. Refrigerate for a couple of hours before serving.

Sauces

Sweet Baking

Savory Baking

Main Dishes

Salads

Soups

Appetizers

Eggplant and Pepper Rolls
Makes 8 rolls

2   **one-pound eggplants**
1   **large red bell pepper**
1   **cup feta cheese or vegan feta cheese**
½   **cup chopped parsley**

Cut the eggplants lengthwise into half-inch thick slices. Spray each slice with olive oil and broil until golden.

Roast the bell pepper until charred. Peel the skin and cut the pepper lengthwise into pieces.

Mix the cheese with the parsley.

Lay out one slice of the eggplant, top with one bell pepper slice, and then place one teaspoon of the cheese mixture in the center. Roll into a one-inch thick roll. Serve at room temperature.

Eggplant with Scallion and Pomegranate Seeds
Serves 4-6

2   **one-pound eggplants**
4   **scallions, diced**
1   **cup chopped cilantro**
1   **red bell pepper, seeded and chopped**
1   **jalapeño pepper, seeded and chopped**
½   **cup coarsely chopped toasted walnuts**
1   **cup pomegranate seeds**
2   **tablespoons pomegranate molasses**
¼   **cup lemon juice**
½   **cup olive oil**
salt to taste

Cut the eggplants into one-inch cubes, place in large bowl and drizzle ¼ cup of the olive oil over the cubes. Toss well and then place them on cookie sheet. Place under a broiler and broil until golden. Remove from the oven and place in salad bowl.

Add the rest of the vegetables, the walnuts and the pomegranate seeds over the eggplant cubes.

Whisk the pomegranate molasses with the lemon juice, the olive oil and the salt. Drizzle this dressing to the vegetables and toss gently.

Sauces

Sweet Baking

Savory Baking

Main Dishes

Salads

Soups

Appetizers

Eggplant with Egg and Garlic Spread
Serves 4

2   **one-pound eggplants**
4   **cloves garlic**
4   **tablespoons olive oil**
2   **eggs**
salt and pepper to taste

Make several cuts into each eggplant. Place on a cookie sheet and broil until charred. (You can also grill the eggplant until charred.) Remove from the grill or the oven and allow it to cool. Peel the skin and mash the pulp.

Mix the mashed eggplants with the garlic, the salt and the pepper.

In a shallow frying pan, heat the olive oil and cook the eggs as though you are making scrambled eggs. Add the eggplant mixture to the eggs and continue to cook for a couple of minutes, stirring often. Remove from the stove and serve hot.

Eggplant and Peppers Spread
Serves 4-6

2   one-pound eggplants
1   green pepper, seeded and finely chopped
1   red bell pepper, seeded and finely chopped
1   yellow bell pepper, seeded and finely chopped
1   jalapeño bell pepper, seeded and finely chopped
1   red onion, finely chopped
1   clove garlic
½   cup chopped dried cranberries
¼   teaspoon crushed pepper
¼   cup lemon juice
¼   cup olive oil
zest of one lemon
salt to taste

Make several thin cuts into each eggplant. Grill or broil in oven until charred. Remove from the heat and allow it to cool. Peel the skin and mash the pulp and place in salad bowl.

Add the vegetables to the eggplant.

Place the garlic in sauce bowl. Add the salt and mash the garlic with salt into smooth paste. Toss the garlic with the chopped cranberries, the crushed pepper and the lemon zest. Add the lemon juice and the olive oil and mix well. Pour this dressing over the eggplant vegetables mixture and toss well. Serve warm or cold.

Sauces

Sweet Baking

Savory Baking

Main Dishes

Salads

Soups

Appetizers

Ratatouille
Serves 4

1	medium onion, finely chopped
4	tablespoons olive oil
2	red bell peppers, seeded and coarsely chopped
1	medium zucchini, cut into 2-inch thick cubes
2	cloves garlic, mashed
2	tomatoes, finely chopped

salt and pepper to taste

Heat the olive oil in a heavy pan and sauté the onions for five minutes.

Add the garlic, the peppers and the zucchini. Stir, cover and cook for 10 minutes.

Add the tomatoes, the seasoning and stir gently. Cover and cook for five minutes.

Zucchini in Tahini Sauce
Serves 4

6   medium zucchinis
1   medium onion, chopped
¼   cup tahini
½   cup lemon juice
½   cup water
2   cloves garlic, mashed
1   teaspoon ground cumin
½   cup parsley, chopped
salt to taste

Slice the zucchini into half-inch thick rounds. Place the zucchinis on a cookie sheet, spray with olive oil and broil until golden. Remove from the oven and place in a baking dish.

Sprinkle the zucchini with the chopped onions.

Whisk the tahini with the lemon juice, the water, the garlic, the cumin and the salt until a smooth sauce.   Drizzle the tahini sauce over the onions.

Cover with aluminum foil and bake in a 350 degrees F oven for 15 minutes.

Remove from the oven. Remove the foil, sprinkle with the parsley and serve hot.

Sauces

Sweet Baking

Savory Baking

Main Dishes

Salads

Soups

Appetizers

Zucchini with Mint
Serves 4

6   zucchinis
1   small onion, chopped
4   tablespoons olive oil
1   teaspoon mint
salt and pepper to taste

Heat the olive oil in heavy pan. Add the onion and sauté for a couple of minutes.

Shred or finely chop the zucchini and then add to the onion. Stir and cook over medium heat for 10 minutes.

Add the mint, the salt and the pepper. Stir and cook for a couple of minutes. Remove from the stove and serve hot or room temperature.

Mango and Black Beans Dip
Serves 6

2	cups cooked black beans
¼	cup olive oil
1	medium red onion, finely chopped
1	red bell pepper, finely chopped
½	cup chopped cilantro
1	large ripe mango, peeled and chopped
½	teaspoon ground cumin
½	teaspoon ground coriander

salt and pepper to taste

In a heavy skillet, heat olive oil and sauté the onion until translucent.

Add the red bell pepper and the cilantro. Stir and cook over medium heat for a couple of minutes.

Add the rest of the ingredients, stir, cover and cook over low heat for five minuets.

Remove from the heat, adjust the seasoning and serve hot.

Sauces

Sweet Baking

Savory Baking

Main Dishes

Salads

Soups

Appetizers

Hummus, Garbanzo Bean Spread
Serves 4-6

2 cups cooked garbanzo beans
4 cloves garlic
¼ cup tahini (see appendix)
¼ cup lemon juice
½ teaspoon cumin
salt to taste

Place garbanzo beans with the garlic and 1 cup of water in a food processor and process into smooth paste.

Add the rest of the ingredients and process until well mixed. Taste the hummus and adjust the seasoning before emptying into a serving bowl. Chill for a couple of hours before serving.

Hummus with Parsley
Serves 4-6

2	cups hummus
½	cup water
½	cup lemon juice
2	cloves garlic, mashed
½	teaspoon ground cumin
1	cup chopped parsley

Mix the hummus with the water and the lemon juice. Add the rest of the ingredients. Chill for a couple of hours before serving. This dip is excellent served with toasted pita chips.

Sauces

Sweet Baking

Savory Baking

Main Dishes

Salads

Soups

Appetizers

Mohamarra: Red Bell Pepper Spread
Serves 4-6

2   red bell peppers, seeded and cut into small pieces
½   medium onion, chopped
1   cup walnuts
2   tablespoons harissa
2   tablespoons pomegranate molasses
½   teaspoon ground cumin
½   teaspoon ground coriander
¼   cup olive oil

Place the bell peppers, the onion and the walnuts in food processor. Using about five on/off turns, process until mixture is coarsely chopped.

Add the harissa, the pomegranate molasses, the cumin, the coriander and the olive oil. Process until finely chopped but not pureed. Serve cold or room temperature.

Sweet and Sour Beet Dip
Makes 2 cups

4   beets
4   cloves garlic, mashed
¼   cup tahini
¼   cup lemon juice
salt to taste

Boil the beets until tender. Remove from the heat and allow to cool. Peel and mash into a smooth paste.

Add the rest of the ingredients and blend well, then serve.

Sauces

Sweet Baking

Savory Baking

Main Dishes

Salads

Soups

Appetizers

Black Olives Tapenade
Makes 2 cups

2	cups pitted Kalamata olives
1	cup walnuts
1	small red onion, chopped
½	lemon, coarsely chopped with the skin
½	cup fresh oregano leaves
¼	cup olive oil

Place the olives with the walnuts, the onion and the lemon in food processor. Using about five on/off turns, process until mixture is coarsely chopped.

Add the oregano and the olive oil and then process for a couple of seconds The spread should be finely chopped, but not pureed.

Green Olives Tapenade
Makes 2 cups

2	cups pitted green olives
1	cup walnuts
1	medium onion, chopped
1	cup chopped parsley
1	tablespoon chopped jalapeño
1	teaspoon oregano
4	tablespoons lemon juice
4	tablespoons olive oil

Place the olives with the walnuts, the onion, the parsley and the jalapeño in food processor. Using about five on/off turns, process until mixture is coarsely chopped.

Add the oregano, the lemon juice and the olive oil and then process for a couple of seconds. The spread should be finely chopped, but not pureed.

Sauces

Sweet Baking

Savory Baking

Main Dishes

Salads

Soups

Appetizers

Labneh: Yogurt Cheese
Makes 2 cups

3	cups plain non-fat Greek yogurt
¼	cup water
¼	teaspoon sea salt

Whisk the yogurt with the water and the salt.

Spoon this mixture into colander lined with fine cheesecloth. Fold the cloth over the yogurt and allow the yogurt to drain overnight, or for eight hours. Spoon the drained yogurt into deep serving bowl, drizzle with olive oil and serve.

Kishkeh: Yogurt Cheese Walnut Spread
Makes 2 cups

2	cups labneh or yogurt cheese
½	cup finely chopped walnuts
½	small onion, chopped
¼	teaspoon dry mint

dash of cayenne pepper

Mix all the ingredients together, spoon into shallow serving platter, drizzle with olive oil and serve.

Sauces

Sweet Baking

Savory Baking

Main Dishes

Salads

Soups

Appetizers

Feta Cheese and Kalamata Olive Spread
Makes 2 cups

1   cup feta cheese
1   cup ricotta cheese
¼   cup finely chopped pitted Kalamata olives
2   scallions, chopped
½   teaspoon oregano
¼   cup olive oil
dash of cayenne pepper

In bowl, mash the feta cheese into smooth paste. Add the rest of the ingredients and mix well.

Rosemary Potato Rounds
Serves 4-6

2	**large potatoes**
2	**tablespoons olive oil**
2	**cloves garlic, mashed**
3	**tablespoons lemon juice**
1	**teaspoon chopped fresh rosemary**
1	**tablespoon parmesan cheese, optional**
½	**teaspoon Spanish paprika**

salt to taste

Cut the potatoes into one-inch thick slices.

Mix olive oil with lemon juice, garlic, rosemary, paprika and salt. Rub the potato slices with the rosemary mix.

Place the potato slices on a cookie sheet, and then bake in a 375 degrees F oven for 40 minutes or until golden. Remove the potatoes from the oven, sprinkle with the parmesan cheese and serve.

Sauces

Sweet Baking

Savory Baking

Main Dishes

Salads

Soups

Appetizers

Potato with Coriander
Serves 4

2   large potatoes, peeled and cut into one-inch cubes
2   tablespoons olive oil
1   medium onion, finely chopped
1   teaspoon ground coriander
salt and pepper to taste

Bring salted water to boil. Drop the potatoes and allow the water to come back to a boil. Allow the potatoes to boil for a couple of minutes. Drain.

In a heavy skillet, heat the olive oil and cook the onion until golden.

Add the potatoes, stir and cook over medium heat for five minutes. Add the coriander, the salt and the pepper. Stir and cook for a couple of minutes.

Spicy Potatoes
Serves 4

4	medium potatoes
3	tablespoons olive oil
¼	cup tomato paste
¼	cup Tabasco sauce
1	teaspoon mustard

salt to taste

Peel the potatoes, cut into one-inch cubes.

Pat dry the potatoes, and then toss them with the olive oil.

Whisk the tomato paste with the Tabasco sauce, the mustard and the salt. Set aside.

Bake in a 375 degrees F oven until golden. Remove from the oven. Drizzle with the hot sauce and serve.

Sauces

Sweet Baking

Savory Baking

Main Dishes

Salads

Soups

Appetizers

Mushrooms with Cilantro
Serves 4

1　pound white mushrooms, sliced
¼　cup olive oil
1　clove garlic, mashed
1　cup fresh chopped cilantro
1　tablespoon lemon juice
½　teaspoon coriander
½　teaspoon chili paste
salt and pepper to taste

In a skillet, heat the olive oil and sauté the mushrooms until golden and the water evaporates.

Add the garlic, the cilantro and the rest of the seasoning. Stir and cook over medium heat for a couple of minutes.

Drizzle with lemon juice and serve hot.

Roasted Peppers with Kalamata Olives
Serves 4-6

2   **red bell peppers**
2   **yellow bell peppers**
1   **cup Kalamata olives, pitted and finely chopped**
½   **scallions, chopped**
1   **teaspoon chopped fresh oregano**
2   **tablespoons olive oil**
1   **tablespoon lemon juice**
zest of one lemon
salt to taste

Broil the peppers until charred. Cool and peel the skin. Remove the seeds, cut into thin slices and place in a shallow serving platter.

Mix the olive oil with the lemon juice, lemon zest and salt.

Sprinkle the chopped olives, the scallions and the oregano over the peppers, and then drizzle the flavored olive oil over the peppers.

Sauces

Sweet Baking

Savory Baking

Main Dishes

Salads

Soups

Appetizers

Artichoke Hearts with Herbs
Serves 4

4	artichokes
1	lemon, sliced
3	cloves garlic, sliced
1	red bell pepper, seeded and finely chopped
1	green bell pepper, seeded and finely chopped
1	jalapeño pepper, seeded and finely chopped
2	scallions, finely chopped
1	cup chopped Italian parsley
3	tablespoons olive oil
¼	cup lemon juice
salt to taste	

Stem the artichokes close to the base. Scoop out the heart and trim the base to form a cup. In a heavy pot, bring 8 cups of water to a boil. Drop the lemon slices and the artichoke bottoms into the boiling water and cook until tender. Drain, and then set aside.

Mix the rest of the ingredients and toss well.

Place the artichoke bottoms on a shallow plate and spoon a little of the pepper mixture into each bottom.

Swiss Chard with Tahini Sauce
Serves 4

1 pound Swiss chard
4 tablespoons tahini (see appendix)
¼ cup lemon juice
3 tablespoons pomegranate molasses
½ cup water
4 cloves garlic, mashed
1 teaspoon ground cumin
salt to taste

Cut the Swiss chard into small pieces. In a large pot, bring water to a boil. Drop the chopped Swiss chard in the boiling water, bring back to a boil and boil for five minutes. Remove from the heat, drain and squeeze excess water.

Whisk the tahini with the lemon juice, pomegranate molasses, water, garlic, cumin and salt into a smooth dressing.

Pour the tahini dressing over the Swiss chard, toss well and serve.

Sauces

Sweet Baking

Savory Baking

Main Dishes

Salads

Soups

Appetizers

Roasted Winter Vegetables
Serves 4

1   medium butternut squash, peeled, seeded and cut into two-inch cubes
1   sweet potato, peeled and cut into two-inch cubes
2   medium parsnips, peeled and cut into two-inch thick slices
4   tablespoons sesame oil
¼   cup raspberry jam
2   tablespoons balsamic vinegar
1   teaspoon finely chopped fresh ginger
salt to taste

Heat the oven to 400 degrees F.

Place the vegetables in a bowl. Mix the sesame oil with the jam, the vinegar, the ginger and the salt.

Place the vegetables in a bowl. Drizzle with the raspberry dressing and toss well. Spread the vegetables out in a baking pan in one layer. Roast in the oven for 40 minutes or until golden and fork tender. Serve hot.

Garbanzo Bean Patties (Falafel)

Makes 40 patties

8	ounces dry garbanzo beans
1	small onion, finely chopped
1	cup chopped parsley
1	clove garlic, mashed
1	teaspoon ground cumin
1	teaspoon ground coriander
1	teaspoon baking powder

salt and pepper to taste
oil for deep frying

Soak the beans in cold water for eight hours. Drain the beans and place in a food processor. Using the on/off button, process until coarsely chopped.

Add the parsley, the onion and the garlic and process until mixture is chopped finely, but not pureed.

Spoon mixture into a large bowl. Add seasoning and mix well.

Stir in the baking powder just before frying.

Shape the mixture into patties two inches in diameter and one-inch thick. Deep fry the patties in hot oil until well browned. Remove from oil and place on a plate lined with a paper towel. Serve with tahini sauce.

Sauces

Sweet Baking

Savory Baking

Main Dishes

Salads

Soups

Appetizers

Skordalia
Makes 3 cups

6   cloves garlic, mashed
4   medium potatoes
4   slices GF white bread slices
½   cup olive oil
½   cup white vinegar
zest of one lemon
salt and pepper to taste

Peel the potatoes and cut in halves. Place the potatoes in heavy pot, cover with water and bring to a boil. Cover and simmer until the potatoes are done and soft. Drain the water and place in a bowl.

Place the bread on cookie sheet and sprinkle with water to make it soft.

Add the garlic to the potatoes and, using a pestle, start to mash.

Add the bread gradually and continue to beat until you have smooth paste.

Slowly add the oil, alternately with the vinegar, and continue to beat until well absorbed.

Add salt, pepper and lemon zest and beat. If the skordalia is thick, add more vinegar and oil. If the skordalia is thin, add more bread.

Sauces

Sweet Baking

Savory Baking

Main Dishes

Salads

Soups

Appetizers

Green Pepper Cilantro and Wasabi Spread
Makes 2 cups

4   **poblano peppers**
2   **green bell peppers**
1   **cup chopped fresh cilantro**
½   **cup wasabi**
1   **teaspoon fresh ginger**
¼   **cup lime juice**
1   **small red onion, finely chopped**
salt to taste

Place the peppers on cookie sheet or grill, and broil or grill until the peppers are charred on all sides. Remove and place in paper bag and allow the peppers to cool.

Remove the peppers from the bag. Peel the skin and remove the seeds. Chop the peppers finely.

Add the cilantro, the ginger and the onions to the peppers. Mix gently.

Whisk the wasabi with the lime juice and the salt. Add to the pepper mix and toss well.

Parsley, Quinoa and Pomegranate Spread
Serves 4-6

½   cup olive oil
1   onion, finely chopped
1   large ripe tomato, diced
3   cups finely chopped parsley
1   tablespoon tomato paste
3   tablespoons chili paste or harissa (see appendix)
2   tablespoons pomegranate molasses (see appendix)
½   cup coarsely chopped walnuts
1   cup red quinoa
salt to taste

Heat the olive oil and sauté the onion until transparent.

Add the tomato and sauté for a couple of minutes. Add the parsley and cook for five minutes.

Add the tomato paste, the chili paste, the pomegranate molasses, 2 cups of water and the salt. Bring to a boil.

Add the quinoa, stir and bring back to a boil. Cover and cook over low heat for five minutes. Remove from the heat and allow the spread to rest for 10 minutes.

Remove from the heat, stir in the walnuts and serve. You can eat this dish hot or cold.

Sun-Dried Tomato and Cranberry Spread
Makes 3 cups

1	cup dried sun-dried tomatoes
1	medium onion, chopped
1	cup dried cranberries
1	cup walnuts
2	tablespoons pomegranate molasses
2	tablespoons chili paste
4	tablespoons olive oil
¼	cup lemon juice
1	teaspoon oregano

salt to taste

Soak the sun-dried tomatoes in hot water for 30 minutes.

Drain and squeeze excess water from the sun-dried tomatoes, and then place in a food processor.

Add the onion to the tomatoes and process until coarsely chopped.

Add the cranberries and the walnuts and process using on/off button for a couple of times.

Add the pomegranate molasses, the chili paste, the olive oil and the seasoning. Process to finely grind, but not very smooth paste.

Vegan Ceviche
Serves 4

12	ounces firm tofu
4	tablespoons olive oil
1	cup chopped cilantro
1	jalapeño pepper, chopped
1	medium red onion, chopped
1	medium tomato, chopped
¼	cup lime juice

salt to taste

Freeze the tofu in the freezer for 24 hours. Remove from the freezer and let the tofu thaw for four hours. Open the box, gently squeeze the excess water and then slice into one-inch thick slices. Place the tofu slices between two kitchen towels and pat gently to dry the tofu more.

In a shallow salad bowl, toss the cilantro with the pepper, the tomato, the onion, the lime juice and the salt. Toss and taste to adjust the seasoning.

Heat the olive oil in a shallow and wide frying pan. Place the tofu slices gently in the pan and sear until slightly golden on both sides. Remove the tofu from the frying pan and place over the vegetables.

Spoon some of the vegetables over the tofu slices, cover and refrigerate for a couple of hours before serving.

Vegan Goat Cheese
Makes 4 2-inches balls

12	ounces firm tofu
1	cup almond milk
½	teaspoon sea salt
½	teaspoon chopped sage
½	teaspoon chopped tarragon
1	clove garlic
⅛	teaspoon cayenne pepper, optional
4	tablespoons dry oregano

Freeze the tofu for 24 hours. Remove from the freezer and allow the tofu to thaw for four hours. Squeeze the excess water and place in a food processor. Puree into smooth paste.

Peel the garlic, pierce a couple of times with knife and place in small cheesecloth. Add the sage, the tarragon and close tightly.

Mix the almond milk with the cayenne pepper and the salt and place in saucepan. Drop the herbs cheesecloth and bring to a boil. Remove from the heat and allow the milk to cool down.

Remove the herbs cheesecloth from the milk and then add to the tofu. Process the mixture for one minute.

Line a colander with two layers of cheesecloth. Spoon the tofu mixture into the cheesecloth. Fold the cheesecloth over the tofu and refrigerate for a couple of hours.

Line flat plate with kitchen towel. Spoon the tofu onto four different spots on the kitchen towel. Cover with another kitchen towel and refrigerate overnight.

Remove from the refrigerator. Wet your palms with water and place one of the tofu balls into your palm and smooth into ball. Roll each ball in the dry oregano and place on the side. Repeat until you finish the rest of the balls. Place in a container, cover and refrigerate. Use this cheese the same as you would use the goat cheese.

Sauces

Sweet Baking

Savory Baking

Main Dishes

Salads

Soups

Appetizers

Vegan Feta Cheese
Makes 2 cups

12   ounces firm tofu
2   cups water
1   tablespoon coarse sea salt

Cut the tofu into one-inch thick slices and place on kitchen towel. Place another kitchen towel on top and gently pat to squeeze as much water without crumbling the tofu.

Mix the water with the salt in saucepan and bring to a boil. Remove from the heat.

Gently cut the tofu into one-inch cubes and place in the hot salted water. Leave the tofu in the water overnight, remove from the water, and place in a container. Cover and refrigerate. Use this cheese in salads, stuffing and in sandwiches.

Vegan "Parmesan" cheese

Makes 1 cup

1   cup slivered almonds
1   cup water
1   teaspoon coarse sea salt
1   clove garlic
1   sage leaf
1   teaspoon chopped rosemary

Place the garlic, the sage and the rosemary in small cheesecloth. Close it tightly, and place it in a pot.

Add water, the sea salt and bring to a boil. Remove from the heat and add the almonds. Allow the almond to marinate overnight in the salted water.

Remove and discard the cheesecloth. Drain the water and place the almonds on cookie sheet and allow them to dry overnight.

Place the almonds in a food processor and grind them for a few seconds, or until they resemble Parmesan cheese. Spoon onto cookie sheet again and bake in 275 degrees F oven for one minute. Remove, cool and then place in a container. Cover tightly and use the same way you would use parmesan cheese.

Sauces

Sweet Baking

Savory Baking

Main Dishes

Salads

Soups

Appetizers

Cheese Toast
Serves 5

1	basic flat bread dough (see recipe)
4	tablespoons olive oil
4	vegan goat cheese balls (see recipe)
2	medium tomatoes, diced
2	scallion, chopped

Line 8" X 14" baking sheet with parchment paper. Moisten your palms with olive oil and spread the dough to cover the baking sheet.

Bake the dough in 395 degrees F oven for 15 minutes. Remove from the oven and allow the dough to cool. Cut the crust into two-inch square pieces. Arrange the squares on a cookie sheet and bake for another five minutes, or until slightly golden. Remove from the oven and cool.

Mix the goat cheese with the olive oil and the tomatoes with the goat cheese. Spoon this mixture onto the baked toasts.

Arrange the toasts on a serving platter, sprinkle with the scallions and serve.

Tomato and Basil Bruschetta
Serves 4

8   ½-inch thick slices black olive bread (see recipe)
2   medium ripe tomatoes, diced
1   cup fresh basil, finely chopped
4   tablespoons olive oil
1   clove garlic, mashed
salt to taste

Mix 2 tablespoons of olive oil with the garlic. Brush the olive bread with the olive oil garlic mixture. Place the bread on a cookie sheet.

Toast the bread in a 395 degrees F oven for a couple of minutes. Remove from the oven and cool.

Toss the diced tomatoes with the basil, the rest of the olive oil and the salt. Spoon this mixture over the toasted bread and serve.

Sauces

Sweet Baking

Savory Baking

Main Dishes

Salads

Soups

Appetizers

SOUPS

Lentil Soup
Serves 4-6

1	**pound lentils**
2	**carrots, finely chopped**
2	**stalks celery, finely chopped**
1	**medium onion, finely chopped**
3	**tablespoons olive oil**
1	**16-ounce can tomato sauce**
1	**teaspoon sage**
2	**bay leaves**
1	**clove garlic**

salt to taste

In a heavy soup pot, heat the olive oil and sauté the onions for a couple of minutes.

Add the celery and the carrots–this will make a roux. Stir and cook over medium-low heat for five minutes.

Add the lentils and 10 cups of water, bay leaves, sage, garlic and salt. Bring to a boil. Boil until lentils are soft but not mushy.

Add the tomato sauce and bring back to a boil. Simmer for ten minutes. Serve hot.

Lentil Cilantro Soup
Serves 4- 6

1	pound lentils
4	tablespoons olive oil
1	medium onion, julienned
6	cloves garlic, mashed
1	cup chopped cilantro
¼	cup lemon juice
1	cup gluten free elbow pasta

salt to taste

In a soup pot, heat olive oil and cook the onions until golden.

Add the lentils, 8 cups of water and bring to a boil. Boil until lentils are soft, but not mushy.

In a small pan, heat the rest of the olive oil and sauté the garlic with the cilantro for one minute, then add the lemon juice.

Add the cilantro lemon mixture to the soup. Adjust the seasoning, and then drop in the pasta. Stir and cook for five minutes and serve.

Sauces

Sweet Baking

Savory Baking

Main Dishes

Salads

Soups

Appetizers

Lentil Soup with Vegetables
Serves 6

1	medium onion, chopped
2	celery stalks, chopped
2	carrots, peeled and chopped
½	cup olive oil
2	cups orange lentils
½	cup short grain rice
2	cups green lentil
4	cups chopped Swiss chard
2	zucchini, diced
4	cloves garlic
1	cup chopped cilantro
¼	cup lemon juice
¼	teaspoon cayenne pepper

salt to taste

In soup pot, heat 4 tablespoons olive oil. Sauté the onion, the celery and the carrots for five minutes.

Add the orange lentils, the rice and 10 cups of water. Bring to a boil, and then cook over medium heat for 30-45 minutes, or until the lentils and the rice are done and mushy. Add salt and cayenne pepper. Add the Swiss chard and the zucchini. Bring back to a boil. Simmer for five minutes. Add more water if the soup is too thick.

Place the green lentil in another pot, cover with water and boil. Cook until the lentil is cooked but still firm. Drain and add to the soup.

Heat the rest of the oil in frying pan. Sauté the garlic and the cilantro for a couple of minutes. Add the lemon juice and then spoon into the soup. Stir and cook for a couple of minutes.

Cream of Split Pea Soup
Serves 6-8

8   ounces split peas
4   tablespoons olive oil
1   small onion, finely chopped
2   celery stalks, finely chopped
3   carrots, finely chopped
2   small potatoes, peeled and diced into half-inch cubes
2   cloves garlic, chopped
½   cup chopped cilantro
½   cup lemon juice
salt and pepper to taste

In a heavy pot, heat olive oil, then cook the onions with the celery and carrots for five minutes.

Add the peas, potatoes and 8 cups of water. Bring to a boil.

Boil the soup for one hour. Add garlic, cilantro, salt and pepper, and simmer for one hour.

Remove from heat, add the lemon juice and then puree into a smooth soup. Serve with corn chips.

Sauces

Sweet Baking

Savory Baking

Main Dishes

Salads

Soups

Appetizers

Vegetable Soup with Olive Bread
Serves 6-8

3	tablespoons olive oil
1	medium onion, chopped
2	celery stalks, diced
3	carrots, diced
1	zucchini, diced
2	medium potatoes, peeled and diced
1	cup chopped cabbage
1	cup chopped kale
1	16-ounce can diced tomatoes
1	16-ounce can cooked kidney beans
1	teaspoon sage
2	bay leaves
½	cup parmesan cheese
	salt and pepper to taste
2	cups olive bread, cubed (see recipe)

In a heavy pot, heat the olive oil and sauté the onion, celery and carrots for a couple of minutes.

Add the diced tomatoes with the juice, 8 cups of water, sage, bay leaves, salt and pepper. Bring to a boil, then add the kale, cabbage and zucchini. Bring back to a boil. Turn down the heat and cook over medium heat for ten minutes. Add the potatoes and cook for ten minutes or until the potatoes are done.

Add the beans and the cheese, stir, adjust the seasoning, and then add the bread. Turn off the heat, stir and serve.

Vegetable Soup with Garbanzo Beans
Serves 6

1	medium onion
6	tablespoons olive oil
2	celery stalks, chopped
3	carrots, peeled and chopped
1	16-ounce can crushed tomatoes
2	potatoes, peeled and cut into ½-inch cubes
1	zucchini, cut into ½-inch cubes
2	cups chopped Swiss chard
2	cups cooked garbanzo beans
4	cloves garlic, mashed
1	tablespoon dry mint

salt and pepper to taste

In heavy soup pot, heat four tablespoons of olive oil. Add the onion, the celery and the carrot. Stir and sauté for a couple of minutes.

Add the crushed tomatoes, 8 cups of water, salt and pepper. Bring to a boil.

Add the potatoes. Bring back to a boil and cook over medium heat for five minutes.

Add the zucchini and the Swiss chard. Bring back to a boil. Cook until the potatoes are cooked but not mushy. Add the garbanzo beans.

In small frying pan, heat the rest of the olive oil. Add the garlic and the mint and cook for one minute. Spoon this mixture into the soup. Simmer the soup for a couple of minutes and serve.

Sauces

Sweet Baking

Savory Baking

Main Dishes

Salads

Soups

Appetizers

Roasted Red Bell Pepper and Wild Rice Soup
Serves 4-6

4	tablespoons olive oil
1	small onion, finely chopped
1	cup chopped celery
1	cup chopped carrots
1	cup wild rice
4	large red bell peppers
1	fresh fennel, julienned
8	ounces tomato sauce
½	teaspoon ground fennel seeds

salt and pepper to taste

Boil wild rice until soft but not mushy. Drain and set aside.

Place the pepper on a baking sheet and broil until charred on both sides. Remove from the oven and place in a paper bag. Cool for ten minutes. Remove from the bag and peel the charred skin and remove the seeds. Puree in a food processor.

In a soup pot, heat the olive oil, then sauté the onions with the carrots and the celery. Stir and cook over low heat for five minutes. Add the julienned fennel. Stir and cook for another minute.

Add the pureed roasted pepper, tomato sauce, four cups of water and the seasoning. Cover and simmer for five minutes.

Add the rice, stir and continue to simmer for another five minutes. Serve.

Butternut Squash Soup
Serves 6

2	2-pound butternut squash	3	celery stalks, diced
2	medium size potatoes, peeled and cut into cubes	¼	teaspoon cayenne pepper
			salt to taste
6	tablespoons olive oil		zest of one lemon
1	medium onion, finely chopped	⅛	cup lemon juice
1	clove garlic, diced	2	tablespoons grated fresh ginger
3	carrots, peeled and diced	¼	cup slivered almonds, optional

With a sharp knife, cut the butternut squash in the middle. Place the cut side on the table, hold tight and use the potato peeler to peel the skin of the squash. Remove the seeds by using grapefruit spoon. Cut the butternut squash into one-inch cubes.

In a heavy pot, heat two tablespoons olive oil and sauté ½ of the onion for a couple of minutes. Add the garlic, stir and cook for few seconds. Add the potatoes and the butternut squash, stir and sauté for couple of minutes. If the potato or the squash stick to the pot, sprinkle with a little water.

Add 10 cups of water, a little salt and bring to a boil. Cover and simmer for 40-50 minutes or until the potato and the squash are cooked and soft.

Puree the potato and the squash with the cooking liquid in a food processor. Place the pureed vegetables back in the pot. Bring back to a boil, stirring often so the vegetables don't stick to the bottom. Add salt and pepper. Adjust the seasoning. Let it simmer.

In a sauté pan, heat the rest of the olive oil and cook the rest of the onion, the carrots and the celery in the oil. Cook for a couple of minutes. Add the lemon zest and the cayenne pepper. Stir and cook for a couple of minutes.

Spoon the cooked vegetables into the pureed potato and squash soup.

Add the fresh ginger and the lemon. Taste and adjust the seasoning.

Spoon the soup into serving bowl, sprinkle with the slivered almonds and serve.

Sauces

Sweet Baking

Savory Baking

Main Dishes

Salads

Soups

Appetizers

Potato Soup
Serves 4-6

2	large potatoes
6	cups water
1	medium onion, finely chopped
4	tablespoons olive oil
2	cloves garlic, mashed
1	6-ounce can sliced mushrooms
½	teaspoon tarragon
½	teaspoon paprika

salt and pepper to taste

Peel the potatoes and cut into one-inch cubes.

Place the potatoes in the water and add the tarragon, the paprika and salt.

Boil until the potatoes are very soft. Remove from the heat and puree until a smooth thick liquid.

In a large heavy pot, sauté the onions in the olive oil for a couple of minutes.

Add the mushrooms and sauté for five minutes. Add the garlic, stir and cook for one minute. Pour in the pureed potatoes and pepper. Stir and simmer for 10 minutes or until the soup thickens, then serve.

Leek, Potato and White Bean Soup
Serves 4-6

4   tablespoons olive oil
1   medium onion, julienned
2   small leeks–use white part only–thinly sliced
½   cup chopped fresh fennel, optional
2   small potatoes, peeled and cut into one-inch cubes
1   cup cooked white cannellini beans
salt and pepper to taste

In a heavy pot, heat olive oil and sauté the onions until golden.

Add the leeks, fennels and potatoes. Sauté for five minutes while stirring.

Add six cups of water, salt and pepper. Stir and bring to a boil. Cover and simmer for 30 minutes.

Add the beans, adjust the seasoning and continue to simmer for five minutes. Remove from heat and serve.

Sauces

Sweet Baking

Savory Baking

Main Dishes

Salads

Soups

Appetizers

Bean and Potato Soup
Serves 4-6

4	tablespoons olive oil
1	medium onion, julienned
2	small leeks–use white part only–thinly sliced
½	cup chopped fresh fennel, optional
2	small potatoes, peeled and cut into one-inch cubes
1	cup cooked white cannellini beans

salt and pepper to taste

In a heavy pot, heat olive oil and sauté the onions until golden.

Add the leeks, fennels and potatoes. Sauté for five minutes while stirring.

Add six cups of water, salt and pepper. Stir and bring to a boil. Cover and simmer for 30 minutes.

Add the beans, adjust the seasoning and continue to simmer for five minutes. Remove from heat and serve.

Bean and Potato Soup
Serves 4-6

1   12-ounce can cooked kidney beans
4   tablespoons olive oil
2   cloves garlic, mashed
1   medium onion, finely chopped
1   celery stalk, finely chopped
3   medium potatoes, peeled and diced
2   medium ripe tomatoes, finely diced
1   vegetable bouillon cube
½   teaspoon sage
2   bay leaves
1   cup chopped parsley
¼   cup Parmesan cheese
salt and pepper to taste

In a heavy pot, heat the olive oil and sauté the garlic, onion and celery for five minutes.

Wash and drain the beans and add them to the vegetables. Add 8 cups of water and bring to a boil. Simmer for 35 minutes.

Remove 1 cup of the beans for later set aside.

Add the tomatoes, potatoes, vegetable bouillon and 2 more cups of water. Bring to a boil.

Add the sage, bay leaves, half of the parsley, salt and pepper.

Cover and simmer for 40 minutes, stirring from time to time.

Add the parmesan cheese and puree with an immersion blender.

Add the saved beans and parsley.

Adjust the seasoning and serve.

Sauces

Sweet Baking

Savory Baking

Main Dishes

Salads

Soups

Appetizers

Vegetable and Pasta Soup
Serves 4-6

4   **tablespoons olive oil**
1   **medium onion, chopped**
3   **celery stalks, chopped**
3   **carrots, diced**
1   **clove garlic, mashed**
1   **32-ounce can tomato sauce**
2   **bay leaves**
1   **teaspoon dry sage**
1   **cup lentils**
1   **zucchini, diced**
1   **potato, peeled and diced**
½   **cup gluten free elbow pasta**
salt and pepper to taste

In a heavy pot, heat olive oil and cook the onions, the celery and the carrots for a couple of minutes.

Add the garlic, the tomato sauce, 4 cups of water, bay leaves, salt and pepper. Bring to a boil.

Add the vegetables and lentils, bring back to a boil, and then reduce the heat and simmer until lentils are cooked.

Adjust the seasoning and add the pasta. Stir and cook until pasta is al-dente. You can add more water if the soup is a little thick. Serve.

Vegan Chili
Serves 4-6

6	tablespoons olive oil
1	medium onion, chopped
1	16-ounce can diced tomato
¼	cup tomato paste
2	cups cooked red kidney beans
1	cup frozen corn kernel, thawed
1	red bell pepper, seeded and diced
1	jalapeño, seeded and diced
2	cloves garlic, mashed
2	cups chopped cilantro
1	tablespoon ground cumin
1	tablespoon ground coriander

salt to taste

In heavy soup pot, heat 4 tablespoons olive oil and sauté the onions for five minutes.

Add the diced tomato, the tomato paste and 4 cups of water, salt and pepper. Bring to a boil.

Add the kidney beans and the corn. Bring back to a boil.

In frying pan, heat the rest of the olive oil. Add the red bell pepper and the jalapeño pepper. Stir and cook for a couple of minutes. Add the garlic, 1 cup of the cilantro, the cumin and the coriander. Stir, remove from the heat and spoon into the beans. Simmer for five minutes.

Spoon into bowl, sprinkle with fresh cilantro and serve.

Sauces

Sweet Baking

Savory Baking

Main Dishes

Salads

Soups

Appetizers

Swiss Chard and Lentil Soup
Serves 4-6

2	**cups lentils**
4	**tablespoons olive oil**
1	**medium onion, chopped**
1	**pound Swiss chard, chopped**
2	**tablespoons garbanzo bean flour**
½	**cup lemon juice**
½	**teaspoon cumin**

salt and pepper to taste

In a heavy soup pan, cover lentils with 8 cups of water and cook for 20 minutes or until lentils are soft.

In a frying pan, heat 2 tablespoons of olive oil, then sauté the onions for a couple of minutes. Add the Swiss chard. Stir and cook over medium heat for five minutes. Add this mixture to the lentils.

In the same frying pan, heat the rest of the olive oil. Add the flour and cumin and mix until you have a smooth paste. Stir in the lemon juice, and then add to the soup.

Add the salt and pepper and continue to cook, stirring often until soup thickens. Serve.

Garbanzo Bean Soup
Serves 4-6

4	tablespoons olive oil
1	medium onion, finely chopped
1	clove garlic
4	cups cooked garbanzo beans
½	teaspoon oregano
½	teaspoon rosemary
1	cup short gluten free pasta
½	cup parmesan cheese

salt and pepper to taste

Heat the olive oil and cook the onion for a couple of minutes.

Add half of the garbanzo beans, 8 cups of water, oregano, rosemary and salt. Bring to a boil.

Puree the rest of the garbanzo beans and the garlic in a food processor. Add the puree to the boiling beans.

Bring the soup back to a boil and adjust the seasoning.

Stir in the pasta and cook until al-dente.

Stir in the cheese and serve.

Sauces

Sweet Baking

Savory Baking

Main Dishes

Salads

Soups

Appetizers

Pumpkin Soup with Fennel and Beet
Serves 4-6

6   tablespoons olive oil
1   medium onion
1   clove garlic, mashed
3   russet potatoes, peeled and cubed
1   16-ounce can puree pumpkin
¼   teaspoon turmeric
½   fresh fennel, chopped
1   small beet, peeled and cut into half-inch cubes
1   tablespoon chopped candied orange peel, optional
½   cup orange juice
1   teaspoon cayenne pepper
salt to taste

Heat the olive oil in heavy soup pot and sauté the onion until transparent.

Add the garlic, the potatoes and 10 cups of water. Bring to a boil. Cover and simmer until the potatoes are done and very soft. Remove from the heat and puree in a food processor. Place the potato puree back in the pot.

Add the pureed pumpkin, the turmeric, the cayenne pepper and the salt. Stir and bring to a boil. Add a little water if the soup is very thick.

Toss the beet cubes with the rest of the olive oil and bake for 20 minutes. Remove from the oven and set aside.

Add the fennel and the orange juice to the soup and cook for a couple of minutes.

Spoon the soup into bowl. Toss the candied orange peel with the beet and spoon in the center of the bowl and serve.

Spicy Garbanzo Bean Soup
Serves 6

5	**cups cooked garbanzo beans**
2	**tablespoons olive oil**
1	**medium onion, chopped**
1	**carrot, diced**
2	**celery stalks, diced**
1	**tablespoon harissa (see appendix)**
2	**cups chopped cabbage**
1	**16-ounce cup crushed tomatoes**
1	**teaspoon sage**
1	**bay leaf**

salt and pepper to taste

In a heavy soup pot, heat olive oil and cook the onion for two minutes. Add the carrots and celery. Stir and cook for five minutes.

Add the harissa and cabbage. Stir and cook for a couple of minutes.

Add 2 cups of water, the crushed tomatoes, sage, bay leaf, salt and pepper. Stir and bring to a boil.

Add half of the cooked garbanzo beans. Bring back to a boil and simmer for 10 minutes.

Puree the rest of the garbanzo beans in a food processor and spoon into the simmering soup.

Stir well, adjust seasoning and continue to simmer for five more minutes. Serve.

Sauces

Sweet Baking

Savory Baking

Main Dishes

Salads

Soups

Appetizers

Cream of Zucchini Soup
Serves 4-6

2	tablespoons olive oil
1	medium onion, chopped
2	pounds zucchini, chopped
1	clove garlic, mashed
½	teaspoon ground cloves
½	teaspoon mint
4	cups vegetable stock or vegetable bouillon
3	cups evaporated skim milk

salt and pepper to taste

Heat the olive oil and cook the onions for five minutes.

Add the zucchini, stir and cook over medium heat for 10 minutes. Add the garlic, mint, cloves and vegetable stock. Stir and continue cooking for another 10 minutes.

Remove zucchini from heat and puree in a food processor until smooth.

Return the zucchini to the pot. Add the rest of the seasoning and the evaporated skim milk. Stir and cook over low heat until hot. Serve.

Acorn Squash Soup
Serves 4

6   ounces lite tofu, drained
1   small leek, washed and chopped
6   ounces acorn squash, peeled and cut into one-inch cubes
1   small yam, peeled and cut into one-inch cubes
6   cups water
2   tablespoons sesame seed oil
1   cube vegetable bouillon
½   teaspoon fresh ground nutmeg
2   cloves
salt to taste

Sauté the leek in the sesame seed oil over low heat for a couple of minutes.

Add the rest of the vegetables and 1 cup of the water. Stir and cook for five minutes.

Dissolve the vegetable bouillon cube in the rest of the water.

Add the tofu, seasoning and the broth water. Stir and bring to a boil. Cover and simmer for 20 minutes or until vegetables are soft.

Remove the cloves, and then puree the soup in a food processor until smooth.

Return soup to the pot. Add water if the soup is very thick. Adjust the seasoning and cook over low heat for five more minutes. Serve.

Sauces

Sweet Baking

Savory Baking

Main Dishes

Salads

Soups

Appetizers

Three Bean Soup

Serves 6

1	cup lentils
3	tablespoons olive oil
1	medium onion, chopped
1	celery stalk, chopped
1	clove garlic, mashed
1	red bell pepper, seeded and chopped
2	cups diced tomatoes
1	cup cooked garbanzo beans
1	cup cooked black-eyed peas
1	teaspoon ground cumin
½	teaspoon chili powder

salt to taste

Heat the olive oil and sauté the onions until soft.

Add the celery, garlic and both chopped peppers. Stir and cook over low heat for five minutes.

Add the lentils and 8 cups of water. Bring to a boil and cook until lentils are soft.

Add the rest of the ingredients. Stir and bring back to a boil. Cover and simmer for 10 minutes. Serve.

Sauces

Sweet Baking

Savory Baking

Main Dishes

Salads

Soups

Appetizers

SALADS

Watercress and Mushroom Salad
Serves 4-6

2   bunches watercress
8   ounces white mushrooms, thinly sliced
¼   cup lemon juice
3   tablespoons olive oil
salt and pepper to taste

Chop the watercress and toss with the mushrooms.

Mix the lemon juice with the olive oil and the seasoning. Pour the lemon dressing over the watercress and toss gently. Serve.

Mushroom and Scallion Salad
Serves 4

4	cups sliced white mushrooms
2	cups chopped scallions
½	cup lemon juice
¼	cup olive oil
½	teaspoon basil

salt and pepper to taste

Place the scallions and the mushrooms in salad bowl and toss.

Whisk the basil with the lemon juice, olive oil, salt and pepper. Drizzle over the salad mixture. Toss gently and serve.

Sauces

Sweet Baking

Savory Baking

Main Dishes

Salads

Soups

Appetizers

Romaine Lettuce and Garbanzo Bean Salad
Serves 4

10   leaves romaine lettuce, chopped
1   bunch parsley, chopped
4   scallions, chopped
2   medium tomatoes, diced
1   cucumber, diced
1   cup quinoa
1   cup cooked garbanzo beans
¼   cup lemon juice
¼   cup olive oil
salt to taste

In a saucepan, bring 1 ½ cups of water with 1 tablespoon of oil to a boil. Drop in the quinoa and cook for a couple of minutes.

Turn off the heat and set aside to cool at room temperature. Squeeze any excess water from the quinoa and place in a salad bowl.

Add the vegetables and the garbanzo beans to the quinoa.

Whisk the oil with lemon juice and salt. Drizzle over the vegetables, toss and serve.

Cabbage and Radish Salad
Serves 4

2   cups chopped green cabbage
1   cup chopped red cabbage
1   cup chopped radishes
½   cup chopped carrots
½   cup dried cranberries
1   teaspoon mint
⅓   cup lemon juice
4   tablespoons olive oil
¼   teaspoon fresh grated ginger
½   cup roasted sunflower seeds
salt and pepper to taste

Place all the vegetables and the cranberries in a salad bowl.

Whisk the lemon juice with the olive oil, the mint, the ginger and the salt. Drizzle over the vegetables and toss well. Sprinkle with the sunflower seeds.

Sauces

Sweet Baking

Savory Baking

Main Dishes

Salads

Soups

Appetizers

Tomato and Scallion Salad
Serves 4

3   **medium tomatoes, diced**
6   **scallions, chopped**
1   **cup chopped fresh oregano**
½   **cup crumbled feta cheese**
3   **tablespoons lemon juice**
4   **tablespoons olive oil**
zest of one lemon
salt and pepper to taste

Gently toss tomatoes with scallions and oregano.

Whisk lemon juice, lemon zest, olive oil and seasoning. Drizzle over the vegetables and toss.

Sprinkle the feta cheese on top and serve.

Cucumber with Feta Cheese and Oregano Salad
Serves 4

6	small pickling cucumbers
2	cups chopped fresh oregano
1	medium sweet onion, julienned
1	cup crumbled feta cheese
2	tablespoons wine vinegar
4	tablespoons olive oil
½	cup coarsely chopped walnuts, toasted

Toss the cucumbers with the oregano and the onions.

Whisk the vinegar with the olive oil and drizzle over the vegetables. Toss gently.

Sprinkle with the walnuts and the feta cheese.

Sauces

Sweet Baking

Savory Baking

Main Dishes

Salads

Soups

Appetizers

Caprese Salad

Serves 4

2   **large ripe tomatoes, sliced**
4   **ounces fresh mozzarella, sliced**
½   **cup chopped fresh basil**
¼   **cup chopped Kalamata olives**
2   **tablespoons olive oil**
1   **teaspoon Balsamic vinegar**
fresh ground black pepper

On a flat serving platter, arrange the cheese in one layer. Arrange the tomato slices on top of the cheese.

Sprinkle the basil and the olives on top of the tomatoes.

Whisk the olive oil and vinegar, and then drizzle over the vegetables.

Sprinkle with black pepper and serve.

Mediterranean Potato Salad
Serves 4

3   medium potatoes, boiled
1   medium tomatoes, finely diced
1   medium sweet onion, finely chopped
1   red bell pepper, finely diced
1   cup chopped Italian parsley
2   tablespoons capers
½   teaspoon dry mint
¼   cup olive oil
4   tablespoons lemon juice
zest of one lemon
salt to taste

Peel and dice the potatoes into half-inch cubes.

Toss the potatoes with the vegetables and the capers.

Add the mint, the olive oil, lemon zest, parsley, lemon juice and salt. Toss gently and serve.

Potato and Roasted Pepper Salad
Serves 4

½   **pound baby new potatoes**
½   **cup capers**
2   **red bell peppers**
1   **yellow bell pepper**
1   **jalapeño pepper**
2   **tablespoons mustard**
4   **tablespoons olive oil**
4   **tablespoons balsamic vinegar**
½   **teaspoon thyme**
salt and pepper to taste

Place the potatoes in a pot, bring to a boil and boil until the potatoes are cooked. Remove from the heat. Rinse with cold water and cut in halves.

Place peppers on a cookie sheet and broil until charred. Remove from the oven, place in a paper bag and seal. Allow the peppers to cool in the bag.

Remove the peppers from the bag; remove the skin and seeds.

Chop the peppers coarsely. Set aside.

Gently toss the potatoes with the roasted peppers and the capers.

Whisk the olive oil with the balsamic vinegar, mustard, thyme, salt and pepper. Drizzle this dressing over the potato mixture and toss gently.

Cover the salad and refrigerate for at least one hour before serving.

Spinach and Walnut Salad
Serves 4

5	cups fresh baby spinach
1	cup coarsely chopped walnuts, toasted
½	cup dried cranberries
¼	cup crumbled goat cheese
3	tablespoons olive oil
2	tablespoons lemon juice

fresh ground black pepper

Toss the spinach with the walnuts and cranberries.

Drizzle the olive oil and the lemon juice over the salad and toss gently.

Sprinkle the cheese and the pepper on top of the salad and serve.

Sauces

Sweet Baking

Savory Baking

Main Dishes

Salads

Soups

Appetizers

Bean Salad
Serves 6

1	cup cooked garbanzo beans
1	cup cooked kidney beans
1	cup cooked corn
½	cup cooked black beans
1	red bell pepper, finely diced
½	cup chopped Italian parsley
4	scallions, finely diced
¼	cup olive oil
3	tablespoons lemon juice

salt to taste

Toss beans and vegetables together.

Add the oil, lemon juice and salt. Toss and serve.

Cucumber and Yogurt Salad
Serves 4

2	cups plain non-fat yogurt
½	cup water
2	small pickling cucumbers, finely diced
1	clove garlic, mashed
1	teaspoon dry mint

salt to taste

Whisk yogurt, water, garlic, mint and salt into a smooth paste.

Add the cucumbers and mix. Serve cold.

Sauces

Sweet Baking

Savory Baking

Main Dishes

Salads

Soups

Appetizers

Bread Fattoush Salad
Serves 4

2	loaves of flat bread (see recipe)
1	tablespoon dry thyme
1	medium tomato, diced
1	medium cucumber, peeled and diced
2	scallions, diced
2	radishes, julienned
1	cup chopped parsley
4	Romaine lettuce leaves, chopped
¼	cup olive oil
4	tablespoons lemon juice
2	tablespoons balsamic vinegar
½	teaspoon dry mint
1	tablespoon sesame seeds

zest of one lemon
salt to taste

Mix thyme, mint, salt and sesame seeds with two tablespoons of olive oil. Brush this mixture on the bread. Cut the bread into one-inch pieces and place on cookie sheet. Toast the bread in a 375 degrees F oven until crisp.

Remove from the bread from the oven and let it cool. Set aside.

Whisk together vinegar, remaining olive oil, lemon zest and salt to make the dressing.

In a salad bowl, toss all the vegetables, then drizzle the dressing over the vegetables. Toss until well coated.

Place the toasted thyme bread over the salad and serve.

Quinoa and Broccoli Salad
Serves 4

2	**cups quinoa**
2	**cups broccoli florets**
1	**cup shredded carrots**
½	**cup raisins**
¼	**cup toasted sunflower seeds**
½	**cup lemon juice**
¼	**cup sesame seed oil**

zest of one lemon

salt to taste

Bring 4 cups of salted water to a boil. Add the quinoa and one tablespoon of sesame seed oil. Stir and bring back to a boil. Cook for a couple of minutes. Remove from heat and allow the quinoa to set for ten minutes.

Squeeze excess water from the quinoa. Place the quinoa in salad bowl and drizzle with a couple tablespoons of sesame seed oil.

Add the broccoli, the carrots, the raisins and the sunflower seeds to the quinoa and toss well.

Whisk the rest of the oil with the lemon zest and the lemon juice. Toss and serve warm or cold.

Sauces

Sweet Baking

Savory Baking

Main Dishes

Salads

Soups

Appetizers

Wild Rice Salad
Serves 4

1	cup wild rice
½	cup shredded carrots
1	cup shredded red cabbage
1	cup shredded green cabbage
½	cup chopped toasted walnuts
½	cup dried cranberries
4	tablespoons walnut oil
4	tablespoons lemon juice
2	tablespoons gluten free soy sauce
1	tablespoon honey

zest of one lemon

Boil wild rice until soft but not mushy. Drain and toss with 1 tablespoon of walnut oil and 1 tablespoon of the gluten free soy sauce.

Mix the vegetables and dried cranberries with the wild rice.

Whisk together the remaining walnut oil with the soy sauce, honey, lemon juice and lemon zest. Drizzle over the vegetable mixture. Toss well.

Sprinkle the toasted walnuts on top and serve.

Garbanzo Bean and Mint Salad with Quinoa
Serves 6

1   **cup quinoa**
1   **cup cooked garbanzo beans**
2   **baby cucumbers, diced**
2   **scallions, chopped**
1   **cup chopped fresh mint**
1   **teaspoon black pepper**
¼   **cup olive oil**
¼   **cup lemon juice**
zest of one lemon
salt to taste

Bring 1 cup of water to a boil. Stir in the quinoa and cook for a couple of minutes. Remove from heat, fluff and allow quinoa to cool.

Mix the vegetables with the beans and quinoa.

Whisk lemon juice with the olive oil, lemon zest and seasoning. Drizzle the lemon dressing over the vegetable salad. Add the fresh mint and toss well.

Sauces

Sweet Baking

Savory Baking

Main Dishes

Salads

Soups

Appetizers

Tabbouli Salad
Serves 4

2	bunches parsley, finely chopped
2	medium tomatoes, finely diced
1	small sweet onion, finely chopped
1	cup quinoa
¼	cup olive oil
½	cup lemon juice
salt to taste	

Bring 1 cup of water to a boil, drop in the quinoa, stir and cook for a couple of minutes. Remove from heat and allow the quinoa to cool.

Add the vegetables to the quinoa and toss gently.

Whisk the olive oil with the lemon juice and salt. Drizzle over the vegetables and toss until well coated.

Nicoise Salad
Serves 4-6

½   pound small boiling potatoes
½   pound green beans, trimmed
2   hard-boiled eggs, quartered
1   head Boston lettuce, torn into bite-size pieces
2   medium tomatoes, cut into 8 wedges
½   cup Nicoise olives (pitted Kalamata olives would be a good substitute)
2   tablespoons lemon juice
2   teaspoons dijon mustard
2   teaspoons balsamic vinegar
4   tablespoons olive oil
salt and pepper to taste

To make the dressing, whisk lemon juice with the mustard, vinegar, oil, salt and pepper.

Place the potatoes in a pot, cover the potatoes with slightly salted water and bring to a boil. Simmer until the potatoes are tender. Remove from the heat, drain, rinse with cold water and peel.

Cut the potatoes in halves and toss with 1 tablespoon of the dressing.

Bring 2 quarts of water to a boil. Drop in the beans and cook for five minutes. Drain and rinse in cold water. Toss the beans with 1 tablespoon of the dressing.

Spread the lettuce in a clear glass salad bowl. Scatter the potatoes and the beans over the lettuce.

Sprinkle the diced tomatoes on top of the potato layer.

Arrange the boiled eggs on the edge of the salad bowl.

Drizzle the rest of the salad dressing on top, then scatter the olives on top and serve.

Sauces

Sweet Baking

Savory Baking

Main Dishes

Salads

Soups

Appetizers

Spinach Salad with Beets and Clementine Oranges
Serves 4

4   cups baby spinach
1   beet
2   clementine oranges, peeled and sectioned
1   cup slivered almonds, toasted
1   tablespoon balsamic vinegar
1   tablespoon lemon juice
4   tablespoons olive oil
salt and pepper to taste

Boil the beet until tender. Remove from heat, rinse with cold water and peel. Cut into one-inch cubes.

Place the spinach in a salad bowl. Scatter the clementine oranges and the beets over the spinach.

Whisk balsamic vinegar with the lemon juice, olive oil, mustard, salt and pepper. Drizzle this dressing over the spinach and toss gently.

Sprinkle with the toasted almonds and serve.

Three-Color Quinoa Salad
Serves 4

½ cup regular quinoa
½ cup red quinoa
½ cup black quinoa
½ cup chopped dried apricots
½ cup cranberries
½ cup toasted slivered almonds
½ cup chopped red onion
½ cup lime juice
6 tablespoons toasted sesame seed oil
⅛ teaspoon cayenne pepper
zest of one lemon
salt to taste

Place the apricots, the cranberries, the almonds, and the red onion in salad bowl.

Whisk the lime juice with the sesame seed oil, the cayenne pepper, the lemon zest and the salt. Set aside.

Place three small pots on the stove. Place the regular quinoa in one pot, the red quinoa in another and the black quinoa in the third. Pour 1 cup of water in each pot. Stir and bring to a boil. Stir again and turn the stove off and let the quinoa get softer for about five minutes. Spoon the three cooked quinoas over the apricot mixture.

Drizzle the sesame dressing over the hot quinoa and toss well. This salad can be eaten hot or cold.

Sauces

Sweet Baking

Savory Baking

Main Dishes

Salads

Soups

Appetizers

Spinach and Beet Salad
Serves 4

6	cups baby spinach
2	medium beets
1	cup chopped green cabbage
4	scallions, chopped
¼	cup lemon juice
½	cup frozen raspberries, thawed
4	tablespoons olive oil

zest of one lemon
salt to taste

1	teaspoon toasted sesame seeds

Boil the beets until cooked but not mushy. Remove, cool and peel the skin. Slice the beet into ⅛-inch thick rounds. Place the beets on a plate and drizzle with a couple tablespoons of lemon juice.

Place the baby spinach in a salad bowl. Toss with the cabbage and the scallions.

Whisk the raspberries with the olive oil, the rest of the lemon juice, the lemon zest and the salt. Drizzle the dressing over the spinach and toss gently.

Arrange the beets over the salad, sprinkle with the sesame seeds and serve.

Sauces

Sweet Baking

Savory Baking

Main Dishes

Salads

Soups

Appetizers

Spinach and Butternut Squash and Candied Walnuts Salad
Serves 4

4	cups baby spinach
1	cup chopped red cabbage
¼	cup cranberries
1	medium butternut squash
1	medium red onion, julienned
1	cup candied walnuts*
1	tablespoon orange marmalade
2	tablespoons mustard
¼	cup balsamic vinegar
¼	cup olive oil

salt to taste

Peel the butternut squash, remove the seeds and cut into quarter-inch thick slices. Place in a bowl, drizzle with a couple tablespoons of olive oil and place on cookie sheets. Bake in 375 degrees F oven until golden on the edges. Remove from the oven and set aside.

Place the spinach with the red cabbage, the cranberries, the red onions and the baked butternut squash chips.

Whisk the orange marmalade, mustard, vinegar, olive oil and salt.

Drizzle this dressing over the vegetables and toss gently. Sprinkle with the candied walnuts and serve.

To Make Candied Walnuts:
Place 1 cup of walnuts in a bowl. Whisk 1 tablespoon olive oil with 3 tablespoons of orange marmalade, ⅛ teaspoon cayenne pepper and ⅛ teaspoon ground cinnamon. Drizzle over the walnuts and toss well. Place on a cookie sheet and bake in 300 degrees F oven until golden. Remove from the oven and allow the walnuts to cool.

Arugula and Lettuce Salad with Orange and Ginger Dressing
Serves 4

2   **cups baby arugula**
2   **cups chopped Romaine lettuce**
4   **scallions, chopped**
1   **cup chopped fresh fennel**
1   **cup cooked garbanzo beans**
1   **whole orange**
½   **cup diced carrots**
2   **tablespoons chopped fresh ginger**
4   **tablespoons lemon juice**
4   **tablespoons olive oil**
salt to taste

Place the arugula, the lettuce, the scallions, the fennel and the garbanzo beans in a salad bowl.

Place the whole orange in a food processor. Add the carrots, the ginger, the lemon juice, the olive oil and the salt. Process until you have smooth paste. Spoon this dressing over the greens and toss well. Serve.

Sauces

Sweet Baking

Savory Baking

Main Dishes

Salads

Soups

Appetizers

MAIN DISHES

Lentil and Rice Pilaf
Serves 4-6

2   **cups lentils**
1   **cup basmati rice**
¼   **cup olive oil**
2   **medium onions, julienned**
½   **teaspoon ground cumin, optional**
salt to taste

Heat the olive oil, and then cook the onions in the oil until golden brown.

Remove half of the onions and set aside. Add the lentils and 8 cups of water along with the salt and cumin. Bring to a boil and cook until lentils are done but still firm.

Drain the lentils and the onion mixture into a pot. Save the cooking liquid. Measure 2 ¼ cups of the cooking liquid and pour into the cooked lentils. Bring back to a boil.

Add the rice, stir and bring to a boil again.

Cover and cook over low heat for 15 minutes. Turn off the heat and allow the rice to rest for 10 minutes.

Scoop the lentil rice pilaf into a shallow serving platter. Spread the rest of the caramelized onions on top and serve. It is best served with the yogurt cucumber salad (see recipe).

Greek Eggplant Mousakaa
Serves 4

2 one-pound eggplants
2 medium onions, julienned
¼ cup olive oil
2 cloves garlic, thinly sliced
1 red bell pepper
1 32-ounce can diced tomatoes
salt and pepper to taste

Slice the eggplants into half-inch thick slices. Place the eggplant slices on a cookie sheet, spray with olive oil spray and broil until golden brown. Remove from the oven and set aside.

Broil the pepper until charred on all sides. Place the pepper in a paper bag and seal. When the pepper is cold, remove from the bag, peel the skin, remove the seeds and cut into thin slices.

In a heavy pot, heat the olive oil and cook the onions until golden. Add the garlic and cook for one minute. Add the diced tomatoes, salt and pepper. Stir and cook for five minutes. Remove from heat.

Remove half of the tomato onion mix and set it aside. Place the eggplants and the broiled pepper on top of the remaining mix, and then spoon the rest of the tomato onion sauce on top of that. Cover and cook over medium-low heat for 25 minutes. Serve.

Sauces

Sweet Baking

Savory Baking

Main Dishes

Salads

Soups

Appetizers

Mushroom with Sesame Paste Sauce
Serves 4-6

2	pounds of white mushrooms
¼	cup olive oil
2	cups cooked rice
½	cup tahini (see appendix)
5	cloves garlic, mashed
½	cup lemon juice
1	cup water
1	teaspoon ground cumin
¼	teaspoon cayenne pepper
2	tablespoons toasted pine nuts

salt to taste

Heat the olive oil in frying pan. Add the mushrooms and sauté, stirring often, until the mushrooms are golden. Add a little mashed garlic and a dash of the cumin. Stir and move from the heat.

To Make The Sauce:
Mix the tahini with the rest of the garlic, the lemon juice, the water, the rest of the cumin and salt. Whisk until you have a smooth sauce.

To Assemble The Dish:
Warm the rice and place in a four-inch deep serving platter. Place the mushrooms on top of the rice. Spread the Tahini sauce on top of the mushrooms and rice. Cover evenly, sprinkle with pine nuts and serve.

Eggplant with Almond Stuffing in Tomato Sauce
Serves 4

2   large eggplants
4   tablespoons olive oil
8   ounces coarsely chopped toasted almonds
1   medium onion, chopped
8   garlic cloves, finely chopped
1   15-ounce can diced tomatoes
2   tablespoons tomato paste
¼   cup pomegranate molasses
2   teaspoons cumin
½   teaspoon coriander
⅛   teaspoon cayenne pepper
¼   cup pine nuts, toasted, optional
¼   cup chopped fresh cilantro
salt and pepper to taste

Slice the eggplant into one-inch thick slices. Place the eggplant on a cookie sheet. Spray with olive oil spray and broil until golden brown.

In a pan, heat the olive oil and sauté the onions until transparent. Remove from heat and right away add the almonds, salt, garlic and a dash of cumin. Mix well.

In a small soup pan, mix diced tomatoes with the tomato paste, the pomegranate molasses, the rest of the cumin, the coriander, the cayenne pepper and salt. Stir. Bring to a boil and simmer for five minutes. Remove from heat.

Place the eggplant slices in baking dish, and then spread the almond stuffing on top of the eggplant.

Pour the tomato sauce over the eggplant.

Bake in a 375 degrees F oven for 35 minutes. Remove from the oven, sprinkle with the toasted pine nuts and the cilantro. Serve.

Sauces

Sweet Baking

Savory Baking

Main Dishes

Salads

Soups

Appetizers

Eggplant with Lentil and Caramelized Pearl Onion
Serves 4

1	large eggplant, cut into one-inch cubes	½	cup tomato paste
¼	cup olive oil	½	teaspoon cayenne pepper
1	onion, julienned	½	cup balsamic vinegar
½	pound sliced white mushrooms	1	pound frozen pearl onion, thawed
6	cloves garlic, mashed	4	tablespoons sugar
1	teaspoon ground coriander	2	cups lentils
1	cup chopped cilantro		salt to taste

Place the eggplant cubes in a bowl, drizzle with a couple tablespoons of olive oil. Toss and place on a cookie sheet. Broil until golden. Remove from the oven and set aside.

Place the lentils in a pot with 6 cups of water. Bring to a boil and cook until the lentils are cooked but firm. Drain and set aside.

In a shallow pan, mix ¼ cup of balsamic vinegar with the sugar. Add the pearl onion and cook over medium heat until the liquid is evaporated. Remove from the heat and set aside.

In soup pan, heat the rest of the olive oil. Add the julienned onion and sauté for five minutes. Add the mushrooms and sauté for a couple of minutes.

Add the garlic, the coriander, and the cilantro. Stir and cook for an extra minute.

Add the tomato paste, the rest of the vinegar, 2 cups of water, the cayenne pepper and salt. Bring to a boil. Taste and adjust the seasoning.

Add the eggplants and the lentils and bring to a boil. Cook over medium heat for five minutes.

Remove from the heat, spoon into serving platter and top with the caramelized pearl onions. Serve.

Eggplant Bundles
Serves 4

2   large eggplants, cut lengthwise into half-inch thick slices
6   cloves garlic, mashed
1 ½ cups chopped parsley
1   cup almonds, finely ground
zest of one lemon
4   tomatoes, diced
1   tablespoon tomato paste
1   teaspoon chopped rosemary
salt and pepper to taste

Place the eggplant slices on a cookie sheet, brush with olive oil and broil in the oven until golden brown. Remove from the oven and set aside.

To make the stuffing:
Mix cloves of garlic with the parsley, the almonds and a little salt.

Place 1 teaspoon of the parsley mixture in the wide edge of the broiled eggplant and fold or roll to make a bundle. Gently place the bundle on a baking tray with the folded side facing down. Repeat until you have stuffed all the slices.

To make the sauce: Mix the diced tomatoes with the tomato paste, the rosemary, 1 cup of water, salt and pepper. Spoon the sauce over the eggplant bundles.

Bake in 395 degrees F oven for 15 minutes. Serve hot or cold.

Sauces

Sweet Baking

Savory Baking

Main Dishes

Salads

Soups

Appetizers

Eggplant Kufta with Toasted Almonds
Serves 4

2   large eggplants
1   medium onion, chopped
1   cup chopped parsley
½   cup chopped cilantro
2   cloves garlic, mashed
1   tablespoon coriander
1   teaspoon chili pepper
1   teaspoon Spanish paprika
salt to taste
1   cup coarsely chopped toasted almonds
1   cup gluten free bread crumbs
1   cup tahini pomegranate sauce (see recipe)

Cut the eggplant into half-inch thick slices and place on cookie sheet. Brush each slice with olive oil. Broil the eggplant slices until golden brown. Remove from the oven and allow the slices to cool.

Place the broiled eggplant in a food processor and puree. Spoon the pureed eggplant into a large bowl.

Place the onion, the parsley and the cilantro in food processor until finely chopped. Spoon the mixture onto the pureed eggplant.

Add the garlic, the spices and the salt. Mix well.

In a separate bowl, mix the toasted almonds and the bread crumbs together.

Moisten your palms with olive oil and make two-inch long and one-inch wide ovals with the eggplant mixture. Roll each oval in the almond mixture, and then place on cookie sheet. Repeat until you are done with all the eggplant mixture.

Bake in 395 degrees F oven for 25 minutes. Remove from the oven, drizzle with the tahini pomegranate sauce and serve.

Cauliflower Garbanzo Bean Stew
Serves 4

1	pound cauliflower florets
4	tablespoons olive oil
1	small onion, chopped
4	cloves garlic, coarsely chopped
1	32-ounce can diced tomatoes
2	medium russet potatoes, peeled and cut into one-inch cubes
1	cup cooked garbanzo beans
1	jalapeño pepper
2	cups chopped cilantro
1	jalapeño pepper, finely chopped

zest of one lemon
salt and pepper to taste

Place the cauliflower florets on a cookie sheet, spray with olive oil and broil until golden. Remove from the oven and set aside.

Heat olive oil in a heavy pot. Sauté the onions in the oil for a few minutes.

Add the diced tomatoes, 2 cups of water, one garlic clove, salt and pepper. Stir and bring to a boil.

Drop the potatoes and simmer for 15 minutes or until the potatoes are cooked but not mushy.

Drop in the cauliflower and garbanzo beans, then bring back to a boil. Cover and simmer for five minutes.

Mix the rest of the garlic with the chopped jalapeño, the cilantro and the lemon zest. Turn the heat off and stir the cilantro sauce into the stew. Serve with rice.

Sauces

Sweet Baking

Savory Baking

Main Dishes

Salads

Soups

Appetizers

Stuffed Zucchini in Almond Cilantro Sauce
Serves 4

4	large zucchini squash	2	cups almond milk
4	tablespoons olive oil	½	teaspoon black pepper
1	pound sliced white mushrooms	½	teaspoon white pepper
1	small onion, chopped	¼	teaspoon freshly ground nutmeg
2	cloves garlic, mashed	½	teaspoon chopped fresh ginger
2	tablespoons corn starch	salt to taste	
1	cup chopped cilantro	1	cup slivered almonds

In a deep pot, bring salted water to a boil. Cut the zucchinis lengthwise in half and drop zucchinis in the boiling water. Bring back to a boil and boil for five minutes. Remove the zucchinis from the water and, with a teaspoon, scoop out the insides of the zucchinis. Place the zucchini halves, cut side up, on a greased baking pan.

To Make The Stuffing:
Heat the olive oil in a pan. Add the mushrooms and sauté until golden. Add the onions, the garlic and salt to the mushrooms. Stir and cook for a couple of minutes. Remove from the oven and set aside.

To Make The Sauce:
Mix the cornstarch with ¼ cup of water. Pour the almond milk into saucepan and mix the almond milk with the cornstarch mixture, the nutmeg, the ginger, salt and pepper. Cook the sauce, stirring constantly, until the sauce thickens slightly. Add the cilantro to the sauce and remove from the heat.

To Assemble:
Spoon the mushrooms into the zucchini halves. Pour the sauce over the stuffed zucchini. Sprinkle with the slivered almonds. Bake in a 375 degrees F oven for 30 minutes and until there are a couple golden bubbles on top. Serve.

Tomato and Quinoa Pilaf
Serves 4

¼   cup olive oil
1   medium onion, finely chopped
1   cup cooked garbanzo beans
1   16-ounce can diced tomatoes
1   cup quinoa
salt and pepper to taste

In a heavy pot, heat olive oil and cook the onions until golden.

Add the diced tomatoes with the juice, 1 cup of water and the garbanzo beans. Bring to a boil.

Add salt and pepper and stir in the quinoa. Bring back to a boil, cover and cook over low heat for 10 minutes. Remove from the heat and serve hot.

Sauces

Sweet Baking

Savory Baking

Main Dishes

Salads

Soups

Appetizers

Zucchini Boats with Quinoa and Almond Mint Stuffing
Serves 4

4	6-inch long zucchini
1	cup red quinoa
1	cup cooked garbanzo beans
1	large ripe tomato, diced
½	red onion, chopped
¼	cup chopped fresh mint
¼	cup lemon juice
6	tablespoons olive oil
2	cloves garlic, mashed
1	16-ounce can diced tomatoes
¼	teaspoon dry mint

salt and pepper to taste

Slice the zucchini lengthwise in half. Drop in boiling salted water. Bring back to a boil and cook for a couple of minutes. Remove, drain and cool. Using teaspoon, scoop the seeds from inside of the zucchini and place in baking dish cut side up.

To Make The Stuffing:
Bring 1 ½ cups of water to boil. Drop in the quinoa, stir and cook for five minutes. Remove from the heat, drizzle with 2 tablespoons of olive oil and toss gently and place in a bowl. Add the garbanzo beans, the tomato, the onion, the mint, the lemon juice and salt and pepper. Toss well. Spoon the quinoa mixture into and around the zucchini cavities.

To Make The Tomato Sauce:
Heat the rest of the olive oil in saucepan and sear the garlic for a few seconds. Add the diced tomatoes, dry mint, salt and pepper. Bring to a boil. Remove from the heat and pour over the zucchinis.

Cover the baking dish with a foil and bake in 395 degrees F oven for 25 minutes. Remove from the oven, remove the foil and serve.

Zucchini with Lima Beans and Quinoa Pilaf
Serves 4-6

1   cup red quinoa
¼   cup olive oil
1   medium onion, finely chopped
1   large zucchini, finely chopped
2   cups frozen lima beans, thawed
2   cloves garlic, mashed
1   cup chopped fresh cilantro
salt and pepper to taste

Heat the olive oil and sauté the onions for a couple of minutes.

Add the zucchini and 2 cups of water, stir, cover and cook over medium heat for 10 minutes.

Add the lima beans, quinoa, garlic, cilantro and seasoning. Stir, cover and cook over low heat for 10 minutes. Keep the lid on and allow the pilaf to rest for 10 minutes. Serve.

Sauces

Sweet Baking

Savory Baking

Main Dishes

Salads

Soups

Appetizers

Zucchini and Garbanzo Beans Stew
Serves 4

5	tablespoons olive oil
1	medium onion, chopped
4	cloves garlic, slivered
1	pound stew beef cubes
1	16-ounce can diced tomatoes
1	tablespoon tomato paste
2	zucchinis cut into one-inch cubes
2	cups cooked garbanzo beans
½	teaspoon mint
½	teaspoon allspice

salt and pepper

Heat olive oil and sauté the onions until golden. Add garlic and beef. Stir and cook for 20 minutes or until beef is done.

Add the diced tomatoes, tomato paste, mint, allspice, salt and pepper. Bring to a boil, and then simmer over low heat for 10 minutes.

Add the zucchinis. Stir, cover and continue to simmer for 10 minutes.

Add the beans and cook for another five minutes or until the zucchini is cooked and the liquid is mostly absorbed.

Quinoa and Swiss Chard Pilaf
Serves 4

¼ cup olive oil
1 medium onion, finely chopped
6 cups chopped Swiss chard
1 cup frozen black-eyed peas, thawed
1 cup quinoa
½ teaspoons ground coriander
⅛ cayenne pepper
salt and pepper to taste

Heat the olive oil and sauté the onion until transparent.

Add the Swiss chard, sauté and cook for 10 minutes, stirring often.

Add one cup of water, the coriander, the cayenne pepper, salt and pepper. Bring to boil.
Add the black-eyed peas and the quinoa. Stir, cover and cook over low heat for 10 minutes.
Allow the pilaf to rest for 10 minutes and then serve.

Sauces

Sweet Baking

Savory Baking

Main Dishes

Salads

Soups

Appetizers

Black Bean Tart
Serves 6

1 ½ cups GF flour mixture for savory recipe (see appendix)
¼ cup cooked short rice, pureed
1 teaspoon ground cumin
½ teaspoon ground coriander
½ teaspoon paprika
⅛ teaspoon baking powder
½ teaspoon salt

4 tablespoons butter
1 cup sour cream
¼ cup chopped fresh cilantro
1 cup cooked black beans
1 cup whole kernel corn
1 cup chopped scallions
½ cup chopped red bell pepper
½ cup shredded cheddar cheese
salt to taste

Mix flour, cumin, coriander, paprika and salt.

Add the cooked rice, the butter and a little water to form the dough.

Press the dough onto the bottom and sides of a 10-inch tart pan with a removable, fluted rim. Bake in a 350 degrees F oven for 10 minutes. Remove from the oven and allow it to cool.

In a food processor, puree ½ cup of the cooked black beans with one tablespoon of the chopped cilantro and the sour cream. Set aside.

Mix the rest of the ingredients, except for the cheddar cheese. Set aside.

To Assemble:
Spread the bean sour cream sauce inside the baked shell. Spoon the bean vegetable mixture on top of the sour cream. Sprinkle with the cheddar cheese. Bake in a 350 degrees F oven for 10 minutes. Remove from the oven, cool on a rack for 10 minutes. Serve.

Broiled Vegetable Pie
Serves 4-6

1 ½ cups GF flour mixture for savory recipe (see appendix)
¼   cup pureed cooked rice
4   tablespoons butter
2   tablespoons olive oil
1   red bell pepper, thinly sliced
1   green bell pepper, thinly sliced
1   medium onion, julienned
1   cup ricotta cheese
½   cup feta cheese
1   teaspoon thyme
½   cup chopped Kalamata olives
1   egg
1   tablespoon sesame seeds
⅛   teaspoon cayenne pepper
salt to taste

Toss the vegetables with the olive oil. Place on a cookie sheet and broil until soft and slightly charred. Remove from the oven and cool.

Mix the flours with the butter, the olive oil, cooked rice and cold water. Mix until you have smooth dough. Place the dough between two wax sheets, flatten the dough into ⅛-inch thick. Remove the top sheet and gently place onto cookie sheet.

Mix the ricotta cheese with the feta cheese, olives and thyme. Spoon this mixture on the dough and gently smooth to cover the circle, except for one inch from the edge.

Spoon the vegetables over the cheese, then fold about one inch of dough around the vegetables to form an edge.

Whisk the egg and brush it onto the dough. Sprinkle with the sesame seeds and bake in a 375 degrees F oven until golden. Remove from the oven and cool for 10 minutes. Serve.

Sauces

Sweet Baking

Savory Baking

Main Dishes

Salads

Soups

Appetizers

Risotto with Eggplant and Cheese
Serves 6

1   **large eggplant, cut into one-inch cubes**
6   **tablespoons olive oil**
2   **cloves garlic, diced**
1   **medium onion, chopped**
1   **large ripe tomato, diced**
1½   **cups arborio rice**
6   **cups vegetarian broth**
½   **cup grated parmesan cheese**
1   **cup diced fresh mozzarella cheese, optional**
¼   **cup chopped parsley**
salt and pepper to taste

Place the eggplant cubes on a cookie sheet, spray with olive oil and broil until golden. Remove and set aside.

In a small pan, heat half of the olive oil and sauté the garlic for a few seconds. Add half of the chopped onions and sauté for few minutes. Add the diced tomato, salt and pepper. Stir and cook over medium-low heat for a couple of minutes. Add the eggplant cubes, stir and cook over low heat for five minutes. Spoon out the vegetables onto a plate and set aside.

Place the broth in a pan, heat and allow it to simmer on low heat.

In another pan, heat the rest of the olive oil and sauté the rest of the diced onion over low heat until soft. Add the rice and stir to make sure all the grain is well coated.

Add a half cup of the broth, stir and cook until well absorbed. Continue adding a half cup of the broth at a time, stirring frequently to prevent sticking. Continue adding and stirring until rice is tender and soft.

Add the tomato-eggplant mixture, the parmesan cheese and the last half cup of broth. Stir well until the cheese is melted and the broth is absorbed. Remove from heat. Sprinkle in the parsley and mozzarella cheese. Stir gently. Serve.

Eggplant Parmesan
Serves 4

2   large eggplants cut into half-inch thick slices
½   cup Eggbeaters
1   cup almond flour
½   cup ground walnuts
¼   cup olive oil
4   ounces fresh mozzarella cheese
½   cup parmesan cheese
4   cloves garlic
1   16-ounce can diced tomatoes
2   tablespoons fresh basil
salt and pepper to taste

Place the eggplant slices on a cookie sheet. Spray with olive oil spray and broil until golden. Remove and set aside.

Mix the ground walnuts with the almond flour.

Brush the eggplant slices with the Eggbeaters, and then slightly dip them in the flour walnut mixture.

Heat the olive oil and sear the eggplant slices until golden. Remove and set aside.

In a bowl, mix the diced tomatoes with the garlic, the basil and salt.

In a small baking dish, place the eggplant slices on the bottom. Top with a slice of mozzarella for the first layer, then layer the tomato sauce. Sprinkle with the parmesan cheese.

Bake in a 375 degrees F oven for 30 minutes. Remove from the oven and serve.

Sauces

Sweet Baking

Savory Baking

Main Dishes

Salads

Soups

Appetizers

Rice with Vegetables, Raisins and Ginger
Serves 4

¼   cup olive oil
½   cup slivered almonds
1   small onion, finely chopped
1   clove garlic, mashed
1   green bell pepper, finely diced
1   red bell pepper, finely diced
1   large tomato, diced
1   cup raisins
½   teaspoon ginger
½   teaspoon nutmeg
salt and pepper to taste
1   cup basmati rice
4   scallions, chopped

Heat olive oil in a heavy pot, and then cook the almonds until golden. Remove the almonds from the pot and set aside.

Add the onion and the garlic to the oil and cook over medium-low heat for 10 minutes.

Add the rest of the vegetables except for the scallions. Stir and cook for a couple of minutes.

Add 2 ¼ cup of water, the raisins, the ginger, the nutmeg, salt and pepper. Bring to a boil.

Add the rice. Stir, and then bring back to a boil.

Cover and cook over very low heat for 25 minutes. Remove from the heat. Allow the rice to rest, and then spoon into shallow serving platter. Sprinkle the scallions and the almonds on top of the rice before serving.

Rice and Eggplant with Tomato and Garbanzo Bean Pilaf
Serves 4

1   large eggplant, cut into one-inch thick cubes
1   medium onion, chopped
3   tablespoons olive oil
1   16-ounce can diced tomatoes
1   cup cooked garbanzo beans
1   cup short grain rice
salt and pepper to taste

Place the eggplant cubes on a cookie sheet, spray with olive oil spray and broil until golden. Remove from the oven and set aside.

Heat the olive oil and cook the onions for five minutes. Add the tomatoes, beans, salt and pepper. Stir and simmer for five minutes.

Remove half of the tomato-bean sauce and set aside.

Spoon the broiled eggplant cubes into the tomato-bean mixture inside the pot.

Spread the rice over the eggplants, and then pour the rest of the tomato-bean mixture and 1½ cup water. Bring to a boil, cover and cook over low heat for 25 minutes. Remove from heat and allow it to cool for five minutes before serving.

Sauces

Sweet Baking

Savory Baking

Main Dishes

Salads

Soups

Appetizers

Rice with Carrots, Peas and Almonds
Serves 4

4   tablespoons slivered almonds
¼   cup olive oil
2   cups frozen peas, thawed
1   cup diced carrots
1   cup basmati rice
salt and pepper to taste

Heat the olive oil and cook the almonds until golden.

Add 2¼ cups of water, peas, carrots, salt and pepper. Bring to a boil.

Add the rice, stir and bring back to a boil. Cover and cook over low heat for 25 minutes. Serve hot.

Sauces

Sweet Baking

Savory Baking

Main Dishes

Salads

Soups

Appetizers

Feta Cheese and Olive Tart
Serves 4-6

½   cup walnut flour
1   cup gluten free flour mixture for savory recipe (see recipe)
½   cup quinoa flakes
4   tablespoons butter
2   tablespoons olive oil
4   tablespoons pureed cooked rice
1   cup crumbled feta cheese
1   cup ricotta cheese
1   cup chopped parsley
1   cup chopped scallions
1   egg
salt and pepper to taste
10   Kalamata olives, cut lengthwise in half

In a bowl, mix the flours and the quinoa flakes with a dash of salt. Add the butter and the pureed cooked rice. Mix well into smooth dough. Add a little cold water if you need to.

Spread the dough onto the bottom and sides of a 10-inch tart pan with a removable, fluted rim.

Bake in a 375 degrees F oven for 10 minutes. Remove and cool.

In another bowl, mix the rest of the ingredients, except the olives, and spoon into the tart.

Arrange the black olives, cut side down, on top of the cheese mixture.

Bake the tart in a 375 degrees F oven or 20 minutes. Remove and serve.

Three Cheese Tart
Serves 4

½   cup walnut flour
1   cup gluten free flour mixture for savory recipe (see recipe)
½   cup quinoa flakes
4   tablespoons butter
2   tablespoons olive oil
4   tablespoons pureed cooked rice
1   cup ricotta cheese
1   cup plain cream cheese
1   cup shredded cheddar cheese
2   scallions, chopped
½   cup diced red bell pepper
¼   teaspoon paprika

In a bowl, mix the flours and quinoa flakes with dash of salt. Add the butter and the pureed cooked rice. Mix well into smooth dough. Add a little cold water if you need to.

Spread the dough onto the bottom and sides of a 10-inch tart pan with a removable, fluted rim.

Bake in 375 degrees F for 10 minutes. Remove and cool.

In a food processor, whip the cream cheese with the ricotta cheese. Spoon into bowl and add the cheddar cheese, the scallions, the red bell pepper and the paprika.

Bake in 375 degrees F oven for 20 minutes. Remove and serve.

Mushroom Stuffed Potatoes
Serves 4

8   medium potatoes
4   tablespoons olive oil
1   small onion, chopped
1   pound fresh white mushrooms
1   teaspoon allspice
1   16-ounce can diced tomatoes
1   tablespoon tomato paste
2   cups water
1   clove garlic, mashed
½   teaspoon basil
salt and pepper to taste

Peel the potatoes, then hollow a pocket in them, leaving a half-inch thick wall. Try not to pierce the potatoes. To prevent a change of color, place the potatoes in cold water with a couple teaspoons of lemon juice until you are ready to use them.

Heat the olive oil in a frying pan and cook the onions for few minutes.

Chop the mushrooms and add to the onions. Stir. Add the spices, and cook until the mushrooms are golden.

Stuff the potatoes with the mushroom stuffing, and then arrange the stuffed potatoes in a shallow baking tray.

Mix diced tomatoes, tomato paste, water, garlic, basil and salt. Pour this mixture over the stuffed potatoes.

Bake in a 375 degrees F oven for 45 minutes. Remove from the oven and serve.

Sauces

Sweet Baking

Savory Baking

Main Dishes

Salads

Soups

Appetizers

Pesto Pasta Mold
Serves 6

12 ounces lite tofu, drained
6   cloves garlic
1   cup chopped basil
¼   cup olive oil
salt to taste
1   pound store-bought gluten free spaghetti

In a food processor, puree tofu, garlic, basil, olive oil and salt into a smooth paste. Spoon the tofu pesto into large bowl.

In a large pot, bring salted water to a boil. Add the pasta and cook until al-dente. Drain the pasta well, and spoon into the pesto. Mix well until all the pasta is coated with the basil-tofu paste.

Spoon the pasta into a bundt cake pan with the pasta. Press the pasta very firmly in the cake pan.

Bake in a 375 degrees F oven for 35 minutes.

Place a flat serving platter on top of the cake pan. Quickly invert the pasta mold upside down. Leave the pan on top for couple of minutes, and then remove the pan. Cut and serve.

Lentils with Mushrooms and Kale Lasagna
Serves 6

6	sheets gluten free rice lasagna
½	pound lentils
4	tablespoons olive oil
1	medium onion, julienned
2	cloves garlic, mashed
1	pound white mushrooms, sliced
2	cups chopped kale
1	cup chopped cilantro
2	tablespoons tomato paste
¼	cup gluten free soy sauce

salt and pepper to taste
| 1 | cup tomato sauce |
| ½ | cup grated mozzarella cheese |

Boil the lentils until done but not soft. Drain and set aside.

Bring water to a boil. Drop the kale, bring back to a boil and allow the kale to cook for a couple of minutes. Remove from the heat, drain, cool and then squeeze excess water.

In a pan, heat the olive oil and cook the onions until golden. Add the garlic and the mushrooms. Stir and cook until soft. Add ½ cup of water, the tomato paste, the soy sauce, salt and the pepper.

Add the lentils, the cilantro and the kale. Stir and set aside.

Bring salted water to a boil. Drop the lasagna sheets in the water and cook until al-dente.

Place half of the sheets in a baking tray. Spoon the lentil and kale mixture on top of the lasagna sheets. Place the rest of the lasagna sheets on top. Spread the tomato sauce on top, and then sprinkle with the cheese.

Bake in a 400 degrees F oven for 25 minutes.

Sauces

Sweet Baking

Savory Baking

Main Dishes

Salads

Soups

Appetizers

Spinach Gnocchi in Tomato Sauce
Serves 4

1   pound ricotta cheese
10   ounces frozen chopped spinach, thawed
2   eggs
1 ½   cups gluten free flour mixture for savory recipe (see recipe)
½   cup parmesan cheese
¼   teaspoon nutmeg
¼   teaspoon black pepper
zest of one lemon
salt to taste
2   cups tomato sauce (see recipe)

Spoon the ricotta cheese into cheesecloth and drain well.

Squeeze excess water from the spinach, and then place the spinach in a mixing bowl.

Add the ricotta cheese, the eggs, the parmesan cheese, half of the flour, the lemon zest and the seasoning. Mix well.

Make one-inch balls from the spinach mixture and dip them in the rest of the flour, making sure they are well coated with the flour. Use more flour if needed.

In a heavy pot, bring 3 quarts of water to a boil. Drop gnocchi into the boiling water, four to five balls at a time. Boil for 2 minutes. Remove spinach gnocchi from the water and place in a 14" X 8" inch baking pan.

Cover with the tomato sauce and then bake in a 375 degrees F oven for 30 minutes. Remove from the oven and serve.

Polenta with Mushroom Sauce
Serves 4-6

2   cups milk
1   tablespoon butter
2   cups corn meal
4   tablespoons olive oil
1   small onion, chopped
1   pound thinly sliced white mushrooms
1   clove garlic, mashed
4   tablespoons Marsala wine
½   teaspoon thyme
½   teaspoon ginger
¼   teaspoon nutmeg
¼   cup heavy cream

Bring 1 cup milk with 4 cups water, the butter and a little salt to a boil. Add the corn meal gradually. Cook the polenta for 30 minutes, stirring often.

Heat olive oil in a separate pan and sauté the onion until soft. Add the garlic and the thinly sliced mushrooms. Stir and cook for five minutes.

Add the Marsala wine, the thyme, the nutmeg, and the ginger. Stir and cook until the wine is almost evaporated.

Mix the corn meal with the rest of the milk and the heavy cream, and then pour over the cooked mushrooms. Simmer over medium heat until the sauce thickens, stirring frequently.

Scoop the polenta onto a flat serving dish and pour the mushroom sauce on top. Serve.

Sauces

Sweet Baking

Savory Baking

Main Dishes

Salads

Soups

Appetizers

Fresh Sauce Pasta
Serves 4

1	pound quinoa short pasta
4	tablespoons olive oil
1	clove garlic, chopped
3	cups chopped scallions, green and white parts
3	medium tomatoes, diced
2	tablespoons chopped fresh basil

salt and pepper to taste

Bring salted water to a boil. Drop the pasta, stir and bring to a boil. Boil the pasta for six minutes or until the pasta is cooked but not mushy.

While the pasta is cooking, heat the olive oil and sear the garlic for a few seconds.

Add the scallions and the tomatoes. Stir for a couple of minutes. Drain the pasta and add to the vegetables. Season the pasta with the salt and the pepper and the fresh basil. Stir and serve.

Vegan Mac and Cheese
Serves 6

4	tablespoons olive oil
1	medium red onion, finely chopped
1	cup chopped carrot
½	cup chopped celery
2	cloves garlic, sliced
½	teaspoon chopped fresh sage
1	teaspoon chopped fresh tarragon
½	cup short grain rice
½	teaspoon turmeric
2	cups water

salt and pepper to taste
6	ounces silken tofu
1	pound quinoa short pasta

In a heavy pot, heat the olive oil and sauté the onion for a couple of minutes. Add the celery and the carrots and continue to sauté for five minutes.

Add the garlic, the sage and the tarragon. Sauté for a couple of minutes and add the rice and the turmeric. Stir until the rice is well coated.

Add the water, the salt and the pepper. Bring to a boil and simmer over medium heat, stirring often, for 10 minutes, or until the rice is cooked. Remove from the heat.

Place the cooked rice in a food processor with the tofu and puree until you have smooth yellow paste. (This is your vegan cheese.)

In a pasta pot, bring salted water to boil, and drop the pasta. Stir and boil for six minutes or until the pasta is al-dente. Remove from the heat and drain well.

Place the pasta in a bowl, add the vegan cheese and toss well. Spoon the pasta in a baking dish and bake in a 375 degrees F oven for 25 minutes. You can sprinkle ground toasted almonds on the top if you like.

Sauces

Sweet Baking

Savory Baking

Main Dishes

Salads

Soups

Appetizers

Vegan Asparagus Risotto
Serves 4-6

1 pound fresh asparagus
1 medium onion, finely chopped
2 celery stalks chopped
2 carrots, peeled and finely chopped
1 clove garlic, chopped
1 teaspoon turmeric
6 tablespoons olive oil
1 pound arborio rice
salt to taste

Place the chopped onion, the celery, the carrot and the garlic in a bowl.

Wash the asparagus and cut about two inches from the bottom. Chop finely and add to the vegetable bowl. Cut the rest of the asparagus into one-inch long pieces and set aside.

To make vegan broth, heat 4 tablespoons of olive oil in saucepan, add the chopped vegetables and cook over medium heat until golden. Add 10 cups of water, salt and turmeric and bring to a boil. Cook over medium heat for 10 minutes. Remove from the heat and spoon into food processor. Puree into smooth stock. Place colander over deep saucepan and pour the stock. Discard the vegetables and place the saucepan with stock on the stove. Bring to a boil, turn down the heat and allow the stock to simmer over very low heat.

In another heavy saucepan, heat the rest of the olive oil. Add the rice and stir to coat. Add 1 cup of the stock and stir well. Cook the rice over low to medium heat, stirring often until liquid is absorbed. Add another cup of the warm stock, cook, stirring often until absorbed. Keep repeating this step until rice is soft but not mushy. Add warm water if you need more liquid. Add the fresh asparagus, stir and serve.

Lentil and Mushroom Shepherd Pie
Serves 4-6

2	cups lentils	4	tablespoons pomegranate molasses
½	cup olive oil	1	teaspoon chili paste
1	pound white mushrooms, sliced	3	potatoes
1	medium red onion, finely chopped	2	cloves garlic, mashed
6	cloves garlic, mashed	½	teaspoon ground coriander
1	cup chopped cilantro	⅛	teaspoon cayenne pepper
2	tablespoons tomato paste	salt to taste	

Wash and place the lentils in a pot, bring to a boil and boil until cooked but not mushy. Drain the lentils and set aside.

Heat 4 tablespoons olive oil and sauté the mushrooms until the water is evaporated and the mushrooms start to get golden.

Add the onions, stir and cook over low heat for a couple of minutes. Add half of the garlic and the cilantro. Stir and cook over low heat for five minutes.

Dissolve the tomato paste in 1 cup water. Add the pomegranate molasses, the salt and the chili paste. Pour this mixture over the mushrooms. Add the lentils. Stir and cook over low heat for five minutes. Spoon the lentils into deep baking dish.

Peel and boil the potatoes until soft. Place the potatoes in bowl, add the rest of the garlic, the rest of the olive oil, the coriander, the cayenne pepper and salt. Mash the potatoes until smooth. Add a little boiling water to make the potato smooth. Cut one tip of large Ziploc bag and fit with cake decorating tip and fill ½ full with mashed potatoes. Hold the decorating bag with the tip lightly touching the surface. Using a steady, even pressure, squeeze small cone shape on top of the lentils mixture. Repeat until the potatoes cover all the lentil mixture.

Bake in a 375 F oven for 25 minutes or until the tips are golden.

Sauces

Sweet Baking

Savory Baking

Main Dishes

Salads

Soups

Appetizers

Quinoa Dome with Walnut Stuffing

Makes 8 domes

2 potatoes	2 cups coarsely chopped walnuts
4 cups quinoa flakes	1 clove garlic, mashed
1 cup boiled quinoa	2 teaspoons ground cumin
2 tablespoons potato flour	1 teaspoon ground coriander
½ cup pureed pumpkin	salt and pepper
1 medium onion cut into quarters	1 teaspoon pomegranate molasses
3 onions, finely chopped	1 teaspoon chili paste or harissa
¼ cup olive oil	(see appendix)

To Make The Stuffing:

Heat the olive oil, except for two tablespoons. Add the chopped onions and cook over medium-low heat for five minutes. Add the walnuts and cook for another five minutes. Remove from the heat. Add the garlic, 1 teaspoon cumin, the coriander and salt. Stir and set aside.

Boil the potatoes in water until cooked and soft. Remove from water, peel and cut into quarters.

In a food processor, place ¼ of the raw onion and ¼ of the quinoa flakes in a food processor and process for a half minute. Add a couple quarters of the potatoes and continue to process until the mixture starts to pull away from the wall of the food processor. Remove and place in a chilled mixing bowl. Repeat until you process all the quinoa and potatoes.

Add the pureed pumpkin and the boiled quinoa to the potato dough. Sprinkle with the potato flour, the rest of the cumin, salt and pepper. Mix and knead until the dough is well mixed.

Moisten your palms with olive oil and cut the dough into 16 balls.

Line cookie sheet with parchment paper. Place eight balls on the cookie sheet with about five inches distance. Flatten each ball into ⅛-inch thick round. Spoon the walnut stuffing onto each round. Flatten each of the extra balls in your palm and gently place on top of the stuffing. Seal the edges gently and try, using your palms, to make a dome shape.

Bake in 400 degrees F oven for 45 minutes. Remove from the oven. Whisk the rest of the olive oil with the chili paste and the pomegranate molasses. Paste this sauce on top of the dome. Serve hot or room temperature.

Mashed Potato with Mushroom Gratin
Serves 4-6

6   potatoes
1   jalapeño pepper, pierced a couple of times
½   cup olive oil
4   cloves garlic, mashed
¼   teaspoon cayenne pepper
1   tablespoon grated fresh ginger
1   large onion, julienned

1   pound sliced white mushrooms
4   tablespoons corn starch
6   cups water
1   tablespoon chopped fresh tarragon
⅛   teaspoon ground clove
salt and pepper to taste
1   cup slivered almonds

Peel and cut the potatoes into quarters. Place the potatoes and the jalapeño pepper in pot. Cover with water and a little salt. Boil until the potatoes are cooked and soft. Remove the pepper and discard.

Place the cooked potatoes in a bowl and mash them into smooth paste. Add a little of the cooking water if the potatoes are dry. Add ½ of the olive oil, ½ of the garlic, ½ of the ginger, the cayenne pepper and salt to the potatoes and salt. Mix well and spoon into deep baking dish. Set aside.

In frying pan, heat the rest of the olive oil. Add the mushrooms and sauté until the mushrooms are golden and the water is evaporated. Add the onions. Stir and cook for a couple of minutes.

Dissolve the corn starch in 1 cup of water. Add the rest of the water, the rest of the garlic, the rest of the ginger, the clove, the tarragon and salt. Mix well. Pour into saucepan and cook over medium heat, stirring often, until the sauce is slightly thickened. Pour the sauce over the cooked mushrooms and mix gently.

Spoon the mushroom sauce over the mashed potatoes. Smooth and sprinkle with the slivered almonds.

Bake in 395 degrees F oven for 35 minutes. Remove and serve.

Pasta Puttanesca
Serves 4

4   tablespoons olive oil
4   cloves garlic, cut into thin slivers
1   12-ounce can diced tomatoes
1   tablespoon tomato paste
½   cup baby capers
½   cup chopped pimento olives
½   cup chopped fresh basil
salt and pepper to taste
2   cups quinoa elbow pasta
2   tablespoons grated parmesan cheese

Heat the olive oil and sear the garlic for a few seconds.

Add the diced tomatoes, the tomato paste, salt and pepper.

Cook over medium heat for five minutes, and then stir in the capers and the olives.

Cook for another five minutes.

Bring salted water to a boil and cook the pasta until al-dente. Drain and toss gently with the tomato olive sauce.

Sprinkle with the chopped fresh basil and the grated parmesan. Toss and serve.

Moroccan Couscous
Serves 4-6

3	cups white quinoa
½	cup olive oil
1	cup medium onion, chopped
2	tablespoons tomato paste
1	28-ounce can crushed tomatoes
½	pound baby carrots
1	zucchini, cut into one-inch thick pieces
1	acorn squash, seeded and cut into one-inch thick pieces
1	16-ounce can garbanzo beans, drained
½	teaspoon cumin
½	teaspoon coriander
1	jalapeño pepper, pierce with a fork several times
salt to taste	

To Make The Couscous:

Heat 2 tablespoons of olive oil. Add the quinoa. Stir and cook over medium heat for five minutes, stirring often. Add 3 cups boiling water. Stir, cover and remove from the heat. Set aside.

To Make The Stew:

In a deep pot, heat the rest of the olive oil and cook the onion until transparent.

Pour 8 cups of water, the tomato paste, the crushed tomatoes, the jalapeño and the rest of the seasoning into a pot. Bring to a boil, cover and allow it to simmer for 30 minutes.

Add the vegetables and bring back to a boil. Simmer until vegetables are tender. Adjust the seasoning, and then add the garbanzo beans. Cook for five minutes.

To Serve:

Mix the cooked quinoa with 2 cups of the stew sauce. Toss and scoop into a shallow serving platter. Arrange the vegetables on top of the quinoa couscous. Pour the rest of the stew in a bowl and serve with the couscous.

Sauces

Sweet Baking

Savory Baking

Main Dishes

Salads

Soups

Appetizers

Garbanzo Bean Stew with Toasted Pine Nuts
Serves 4-6

5	cups cooked garbanzo beans
1	cup tahini paste
1	cup lemon juice
5	cloves garlic, mashed
1	tablespoon ground cumin

zest of one lemon
salt to taste

1	cup toasted pine nuts

In a bowl, whisk the tahini with the lemon juice, the garlic, half of the cumin, the lemon zest and salt. Whisk until you have smooth paste. If the sauce is very thick, add ½ cup of water and whisk more. Set aside.

Place the garbanzo beans in a pot with the cooking water. You should have 4 cups of liquid. Add a little of the mashed garlic, half of the cumin and salt. Bring to a boil. Adjust the seasoning and pour into a deep serving bowl.

Spoon the tahini lemon sauce evenly over the garbanzo beans. Stir gently and sprinkle with the toasted pine nuts and serve. This dish goes well with rice or mashed potatoes.

Bread Gratin with Black Olive and Scallions

Serves 4-6

2   loaves gluten free olive bread (see recipe)
8   large tomatoes
4   cups chopped scallions
1   cup chopped Kalamata olives
1   cup shredded Gruyère cheese
1   clove garlic, mashed
salt and pepper to taste

Cut the bread into one-inch cubes.

Place 2 tomatoes in a food processor and process until smooth. Chop the rest of the tomatoes and set aside.

Place half of the bread in deep baking dish. Mix the chopped tomatoes with the chopped scallions and the chopped Kalamata olives. Spoon half of the mixture over the bread.

Place the rest of the bread over the vegetable mixture and then cover with the rest of the vegetable mixture.

Spread the cheese over the vegetables.

Mix the pureed tomatoes with the garlic, salt and pepper.

Bake in 400 degrees F oven for 25 minutes.

Sauces

Sweet Baking

Savory Baking

Main Dishes

Salads

Soups

Appetizers

Rice Kibbeh with Cherry Stuffing
Serves 4-6

4	cups chopped onions
2	cups dried cherries
2	cloves garlic, mashed
1	jalapeño pepper, chopped
¼	cup tamarind juice
2	cups cooked short-grain white rice
2	cups yellow corn meal
½	cup olive oil
⅛	teaspoon cayenne pepper
1	teaspoon Spanish paprika

salt to taste
½ cup pine nuts

To make the stuffing:

Heat ¼ cup of the olive oil and sauté the onions until transparent. Add the cherries, the garlic, the jalapeño and the tamarind juice and salt. Cook over medium heat for five minutes. Spoon the stuffing into baking tray.

To make the rice kibbeh: Mix the cooked rice with the yellow corn meal, the rest of the olive oil, the cayenne pepper, the Spanish paprika and salt. Mix well and cut into six-inch balls.

Moisten your palms with olive oil and flatten each ball into ½-inch thick circle. Place the circle on top of the onion cherry stuffing. Repeat until you finish flatten five of the balls. Use the last ball to patch the kibbeh topping. Smooth the rice kibbeh, sprinkle with the pine nuts and cut into two-inch squares.

Bake in 395 degrees F oven for 35-40 minutes and until the rice is slightly golden.

Stuffed Artichoke Cups
Serves 4

8	artichokes, or 8 frozen artichoke bottoms
1	lemon, sliced
4	cloves garlic, sliced
4	tablespoons olive oil
1	onion, thinly sliced
1	red bell pepper, thinly sliced
½	fresh fennel, thinly sliced
1	tablespoon corn starch
2	cups frozen sweet peas, thawed
1	cup fresh or frozen diced carrots
1	teaspoon grated fresh ginger
¼	teaspoon turmeric or saffron
⅛	teaspoon chili powder, optional

zest of one lemon

salt and pepper to taste

Stem the artichokes close to the base. Scoop out the choke and trim the base to form a cup.

In a heavy pot, bring 8 cups of water, the garlic and the lemon slices to a boil. Drop the artichoke bottoms into the boiling water and cook until tender. Drain and set aside. If you are using frozen artichoke bottoms, defrost and place on the plate.

Mix the cornstarch with ¼ cup of cold water and set aside. Heat the olive oil in a saucepan. Add the onion, the pepper and the fennel. Sauté the vegetables for a couple of minutes. Add the cornstarch mixture, 6 cups of water, the ginger, the lemon zest, the turmeric, the chili powder and salt. Cook, stirring often, until the sauce is slightly thickened. Remove from the stove and set aside.

Place the artichoke cups on a shallow plate. Mix the peas and the carrots, and spoon into the cups. Spoon the onion fennel sauce over the stuffed cups. Grate more fresh ginger on the top and bake in 395 degrees F oven for 30 minutes. Serve.

Sauces

Sweet Baking

Savory Baking

Main Dishes

Salads

Soups

Appetizers

Three Colors Mashed Potato Casserole
Serves 4-6

6	large baking potatoes, peeled and placed in cold water	1	beet, peeled and chopped
1	cup olive oil	1	teaspoon ground coriander
3	cloves garlic	½	teaspoon turmeric
2	teaspoons finely chopped ginger		lemon zest
			salt and pepper to taste

Place two peeled potatoes in a small pot. Add lemon zest, salt and water. Bring to a boil and continue to boil until the potatoes are soft. Remove from the stove and set aside.

Place two other potatoes in another small pot. Add one teaspoon of the fresh ginger, the turmeric, salt and water. Bring to a boil and continue to boil until the potatoes are soft. Remove from the stove and set aside.

Place the last of the potatoes in another small pot. Add the beet, the salt and the water. Bring to a boil and continue to boil until the potatoes are soft. Remove from the stove and set aside.

In small bowl, mash one garlic clove. Add the plain potatoes, a little of the boiling water, 1/3 of the olive oil, salt and pepper. Mash until smooth. Spoon the mashed potatoes into shallow baking dish. Smooth and set aside.

In another bowl, mash one garlic clove, add the pinkish potatoes, the boiled beet, chili paste, coriander, 1/3 of the olive oil and salt. Mash until you have reddish mashed potato. Spoon this potato mix over the plain potatoes about one-inch thick. Smooth and set aside.

In another bowl, mash the last garlic clove, the yellow potatoes, the rest of the ginger, the lemon zest, the rest of the olive oil and salt. Mash until smooth. Spoon the yellow mashed potatoes over the red potato and smooth.

Bake in a 395 degrees F oven for 35 minutes. Serve hot.

Potato and Artichoke Casserole
Serves 4

6	large baking potatoes
6	cloves garlic, mashed
½	teaspoon paprika
2	tablespoons olive oil
1	pound frozen artichoke pieces, thawed
¼	cup capers
1	cup chopped roasted red bell pepper
1	cup chopped scallions
4	cups roasted bell pepper and tahini sauce (see recipe)

To Make The Potatoes:

Peel the potatoes and cut them into one-inch cubes. Add a quarter of the mashed garlic, the paprika and the olive oil. Toss well, place in baking dish and bake in a 375 F oven for 25 minutes. The potatoes should be done but not dry. Remove from the oven and set aside.

Place the potatoes in deep serving tray. Place the artichokes between the potatoes. Sprinkle with capers and roasted bell peppers.

Bring the sauce to boil and spoon it over the potatoes and then sprinkle with the scallions. Serve hot or room temperature.

Sauces

Sweet Baking

Savory Baking

Main Dishes

Salads

Soups

Appetizers

Sweet Peas and Artichoke Stew
Serves 4

1	pound frozen sweet peas, thawed
1	pound frozen artichoke pieces, thawed
6	tablespoons olive oil
½	pound carrots, diced
1	medium onion, chopped
1	16-ounce can diced tomatoes
1	6-ounce can tomato paste
5	cloves garlic, chopped
1	cup chopped fresh cilantro
¼	teaspoon crushed red pepper

salt to taste

Heat 4 tablespoons of olive oil in heavy pan. Cook the onion for a couple of minutes. Add the carrots and sauté for a few minutes. Add the diced tomatoes, the tomato paste, 4 cups of water, crushed red pepper and salt. Stir and bring to a boil. Cover and simmer for another five minutes.

In separate pan, heat the rest of the olive oil and sauté the garlic and the cilantro in the olive oil. Remove from heat and add to the simmering tomato sauce.

Add the sweet peas and the artichokes. Bring back to a boil, cover and cook over medium heat for another five minutes. Serve.

Vegan Spanakopita

Serves 4-6

2	pounds fresh spinach, chopped
1	medium onion, julienned
6	tablespoons olive oil
1	cup crumbled vegan feta (see recipe)
1	cup vegan goat cheese (see recipe)
¼	teaspoon black pepper
1 ½	cup gluten free flour mixture for savory recipe (see recipe)
4	tablespoons vegan butter
3	tablespoons pureed cooked rice
½	teaspoon salt
¼	teaspoon baking powder

To Make The Spinach:

Heat 4 tablespoons of olive oil in pan. Add the spinach, stir and cook couple minutes or until the leaves are wilted. Remove from the heat and spoon into colander. Allow the liquid to drain from the spinach. Spoon the spinach into a bowl and add the crumbled feta, the goat cheese and the black pepper. Mix well and then spoon into 8" X 11" baking pan.

To Make The Crust:

In a bowl, mix the flour with the salt and the baking powder. Add the butter, the rest of the olive oil, the rice puree and a couple tablespoons of cold water. Mix well into smooth dough.

Place wax paper on board, brush with olive oil, and then place the dough on top of the wax paper. Grease another wax paper on top. Gently and with the palm of your hand, push down and spread until you have ⅛-inch thick dough. Remove the top sheet and gently, but quickly, flip the dough on top of the spinach. If the dough breaks, just patch it. Cut the edges and then gently cut the crust into diamonds or square shapes.

Bake in 395 degrees F oven for 35 minutes and until it is a little golden. Remove from the oven, and allow the spanakopita to rest for 10 minutes. Serve.

Sauces

Sweet Baking

Savory Baking

Main Dishes

Salads

Soups

Appetizers

SAVORY BAKING

Simple Flat Bread
Makes 6 loaves

1	cup cooked short grain rice (see appendix)
2	cups quinoa flakes
	dash of salt
2	tablespoons of olive oil

Place the still hot sticky cooked rice in a bowl. Add the flakes and the salt and mix until you have soft dough.

Divide the dough into 6 balls. Moisten your palms in the olive oil and flatten each ball into 6-inch circle and place on cookie sheet.

Bake in 400 degrees F oven for 7-10 minutes until the edges start to turn golden. Remove from the oven and allow the bread to cool. Wrap the bread to prevent drying.

Corn Flat Bread
Makes 6 loaves

1   cup quinoa flakes
1   cup maiz corn flour
½   cup water
1   teaspoon salt
3   tablespoons olive oil

Moisten the quinoa flakes with the water.

Add the corn flour and the salt. Mix well. Make into 6 balls.

Moisten your palms with the olive oil and flatten each ball into 6-inches flat bread.

Place all bread on greased cookie sheet and bake in a 400 degrees F oven for ten minutes or until golden.

Sauces

Sweet Baking

Savory Baking

Main Dishes

Salads

Soups

Appetizers

Corn Bread
Makes 1 loaf

1　cup gluten free savory flour (see appendix)
1　cup yellow corn meal
½　cup hazelnut flour
¼　cup sugar
2　teaspoon baking powder
½　teaspoon salt
1　cup skim milk
¼　cup vegetable oil
¼　cup pureed candied orange peel (see recipe)
1　egg

Heat oven to 400 degrees F.

Grease 9-inch pan.

Mix dry ingredients and set aside.

Beat the egg with the sugar, and then add the oil, the milk and the pureed orange.
Mix well.

Add dry ingredients to the liquid mixture and mix until dry ingredients are fully moistened.

Pour the batter into the pan and bake for 20-30 minutes or until light golden brown and knife inserted in the center comes out clean. Serve warm.

Rosemary Focaccias
Makes 2 loaves

1   cup pureed cooked rice (see appendix)
¼   cup olive oil
1   egg
½   cup buttermilk
1   cup GF flour mixture for savory recipe (see appendix)
1   cup quinoa flakes
1   tablespoon chopped fresh rosemary
2   tablespoons olive oil
salt to taste

Whisk the egg and mix with the olive oil and the buttermilk.

Add the pureed cooked rice to form a paste.

Mix the flour with the quinoa, the salt and the rosemary.

Add the flour to the pureed cooked rice mixture and gently fold to smooth dough.

Cut the dough into 2 balls, flatten each ball on cookies sheet and then brush with olive oil. Bake in 400F oven until golden, about 20 minutes.

Sauces

Sweet Baking

Savory Baking

Main Dishes

Salads

Soups

Appetizers

Onion Focaccia
Serves 8

1	**basic rosemary focaccia**
4	**tablespoons olive oil**
2	**red onions, thinly sliced**
4	**tablespoons Parmesan cheese**

Place the dough in greased bowl, cover and allow it to rise for 30 minutes.

Rub the onions with 2 tablespoons of olive oil and dash of sea salt.

On a lightly floured surface, roll the dough into 1-inch thick round.

Place the dough on greased pizza sheet. Brush the top of the dough with the rest of the olive oil and then spread the onions on top.

Bake in 400 degrees F oven for 30 minutes or until golden.

Remove from the oven, sprinkle with the Parmesan cheese and serve.

Pizza Crust (1)
Makes 1 12-inch crust

1	**cup quinoa flakes**
1	**cup quinoa flour**
1	**cup pureed cooked rice (see appendix)**
1	**teaspoon sea salt**
1	**teaspoon baking soda**
¼	**teaspoon baking powder**
¼	**cup water**
4	**tablespoons olive oil**
1	**clove garlic, mashed**

Mix the quinoa flakes with the flour, the salt, the baking powder and the baking soda.

Mix the water with three tablespoons of olive oil and the garlic. Add to the flour mixture.

Add the cooked rice and knead. If the dough is dry, add more water until the dough is smooth.

Grease a 12-inch pizza pan with olive oil and then press the dough into the pan. Drizzle the rest of the olive oil over the crust and smooth with your palm.

Bake the crust for 10 minutes.

Remove from the oven. Add the tomato sauce and toppings and bake for 20 minutes.

Sauces

Sweet Baking

Savory Baking

Main Dishes

Salads

Soups

Appetizers

Pizza Crust (2)
Makes 2 8-inch crusts

1	cup pureed cooked rice (see appendix)
1	cup buttermilk
1	tablespoon yeast
½	teaspoon sugar
1	egg
¼	cup olive oil
2	cup GF flour mixture for savory recipe (see appendix)
1	cup quinoa flakes
1	teaspoon sea salt

Stir the sugar and the yeast in ¼ cup of warm water. Allow the mixture to rest for 5 minutes and the yeast is activated. Add the buttermilk and mix gently.

Whisk the egg and mix with the olive oil. Add to the buttermilk mixture and the pureed rice and mix well.

Toss the flour mixture with the quinoa flakes and salt. And add ½ cup a time to the egg buttermilk mixture. Mix and knead until you have smooth dough.

Grease 2 8-inch pizza pans with olive oil. Place half of the dough in each pan and press gently into the pan until you have smooth round 1-inch thick crust.

Bake in 350 degrees F oven for 10 minutes. Remove from the oven and either add the tomato sauce and topping and bake the pizza or cool, wrap and freeze for anytime you feel like having a pizza.

Pizza crust (3)
Makes 2 8-inch crusts

2	cups GF savory flour (see appendix)
½	cup quinoa flakes
1	tablespoon baking powder
1	teaspoon baking soda
½	teaspoon salt
2	eggs
1 ½	cups buttermilk
2	tablespoons sugar
2	tablespoons melted butter

Mix all the dry ingredients together.

Mix the sugar and the butter into smooth paste.

Whisk the eggs and add to the butter sugar paste. Add the buttermilk and whisk.

Add the dry mixture into the buttermilk mixture ½ cup at a time. Gently mix until you have smooth dough.

Grease 2 8-inch pizza pan with olive oil. Place half of the dough in each pan and press gently into the pan until you have smooth round 1-inch thick crust.

Bake in 350 degrees F oven for 10 minutes. Remove from the oven and either add the tomato sauce and toppings and bake the pizza or cool, wrap and freeze for anytime you feel like having a pizza.

Sauces

Sweet Baking

Savory Baking

Main Dishes

Salads

Soups

Appetizers

Pita Bread/Pizza Crust
Makes about 8 loaves of bread or 2 pizza crusts

2	cups GF flour mixture for savory recipe (see appendix)
½	cup white quinoa
¼	cup cooked and pureed white rice
1	teaspoon sugar
1	tablespoon yeast
3	tablespoons olive oil
1	dash of salt

Place pizza stone in the middle shelf of the oven and heat the oven to 450 F.

Place the quinoa in pot with 1½ cups water. Bring to boil and cook until quinoa is almost overcooked and there is no water left. Remove from the stove and set aside.

Mix the yeast with ½ cup of warm water and 1 teaspoon of sugar and allow the yeast to get active and double in size.

Place the GF flour in mixer, add the cooked quinoa and the yeast and mix using the dough hook. Add the olive oil and ½ cup of warm water. Knead into smooth dough. Sprinkle the salt and continue kneading.

Remove from the mixer. Moisten your palm with olive oil and knead further into smooth dough.

Dust table with GF flour and cut the dough into 8 balls. Dust each dough and flatten into ⅛-inch thick rounds. Place on parchment paper and then place on the hot baking stone or on a baking sheet in the hot oven (if you don't have a pizza stone). The bread will cook in a couple of minutes. Remove from the oven and allow it to cool down before you pack the bread.

To Make Pizza Crust:
Divide the dough into two balls. Moisten your palms with olive oil and flatten into 1/2-inch thick rounds. Bake in the oven for 5 minutes and then remove from the oven and top with any sauce or topping you would like.

French Baguette
Makes 2 loaves

1	cup pureed cooked rice (see appendix)
1	cup buttermilk
1	tablespoon yeast
½	teaspoon sugar
1	egg
¼	cup olive oil
2	cup GF flour mixture for savory recipe (see appendix)
1	cup quinoa flakes
1	teaspoon sea salt

Stir the sugar and the yeast in ¼ cup of warm water. Allow the mixture to rest for 5 minutes until the yeast is activated. Add the buttermilk and mix gently.

Whisk the egg and mix with the olive oil. Add to the buttermilk mixture and the pureed rice and mix well.

Toss the flour mixture with the quinoa flakes and salt. And add ½ cup a time to the egg buttermilk mixture. Mix and knead until you have smooth dough.

Cut into 2 balls and shape each one into baguette shape about 8-inch long and about 3 inch-thick. Brush with water and bake in 400 degrees F oven for 25 minutes.

Sauces

Sweet Baking

Savory Baking

Main Dishes

Salads

Soups

Appetizers

French Bread
Makes 2 loaves

2	cups GF flour mixture for savory recipe (see appendix)
½	cup quinoa flakes
1	tablespoon baking powder
½	teaspoon sea salt
1 ½	cup plain Greek yogurt
2	eggs
1	cup buttermilk
½	cup pureed cooked rice (see recipe)
6	tablespoons melted butter, at room temperature

Mix all the dry ingredients in one bowl.

Place the Greek yogurt in a bowl, add the buttermilk and whisk well. Whisk the eggs and then add to the yogurt mixture. Mix in the pureed rice.

Start to add the dry mixture to the yogurt mixture ½ cup a time until you have sticky dough. Dust your palms with GF flour and shape into two 2-inch thick loaves. Place the loaves on cookie sheet or French bread baking pan. Moisten with a little water. Leave to rise for 10 minutes.

Bake in 395 degrees F oven for 45 minutes or until golden. Remove from the oven, brush with melted butter and enjoy.

Hamburger Buns
Makes 12 buns

2	cups GF savory all purpose flour (see appendix)
½	cup quinoa flour
1	teaspoon baking powder
1	teaspoon baking soda
½	teaspoon baking salt
2	cups plain yogurt
3	eggs
¼	cup sugar
8	tablespoons butter

Mix the dry ingredients, except for the sugar, together.

Mix the sugar with the butter until you have smooth paste. Whisk the eggs and add to the butter sugar mixture.

Add the yogurt to the egg mixture and mix well.

Add the dry ingredients to the yogurt egg mixture ½ cup at time. Mix to coarse dough. Moisten your palms with little water and knead to smooth dough.

Cut the dough into 12 balls. Moisten your palms with olive oil and smooth each ball and then place on cookie sheet.

Allow the dough to rest for 10 minutes.

Bake in 400 degrees F oven for 10-15 minutes or the buns are golden and done. Remove and cool for 15 minutes before slicing.

Sauces

Sweet Baking

Savory Baking

Main Dishes

Salads

Soups

Appetizers

Dinner Rolls
Makes 10 rolls

2   cups GF flour mixture for savory recipe (see appendix)
½   cup quinoa flakes
1   tablespoon baking powder
1   teaspoon baking soda
½   teaspoon salt
2   eggs
1 ½ cups buttermilk
2   tablespoons sugar
2   tablespoons melted butter

Mix all the dry ingredients together.

Mix the sugar and the butter into smooth paste.

Whisk the eggs and add to the butter sugar paste. Add the buttermilk and whisk.

Add the dry mixture into the buttermilk mixture ½ cup at a time. Gently mix until you have smooth dough.

Cut the dough into 10 3-inch thick rolls and shape into an oval shape and place on cookie sheet.

Rest the dough for 15 minutes.

Bake in 395 degrees F oven for 25 minutes. Take out of the oven and brush with melted butter. Place the tray back in the oven and bake for 3 minutes.

Buttermilk Biscuit
Makes 8 biscuits

2	cups GF flour mixture for savory recipe (see appendix)
¼	cup buttermilk powder
2	tablespoons sugar
2	teaspoons baking powder
1	teaspoon baking soda
¼	teaspoon caraway seeds
8	tablespoon chilled butter
1 ¼	cup heavy cream

Mix the dry ingredients together.

Add the chilled butter and mix until you have coarse meal. You can use the food processor to mix the butter with the flour mixture.

Place the flour butter mixture in a bowl, add 1 cup of heavy cream and gently mix until you have tough dough. Moisten your palms with little heavy cream and start to knead. Repeat couple times until you have smooth dough. Remove the dough and place on gently floured surface.

Roll the dough into 1-inch thick round. Dip 2 ½ inch biscuit cutter in GF flour and cut 8 biscuits. Gently remove the biscuits and place on baking sheet about 2 inches apart.

Bake in 400 degrees F oven for 12-15 minutes. Remove from the oven and cool for 5 minutes before serving.

Sauces

Sweet Baking

Savory Baking

Main Dishes

Salads

Soups

Appetizers

Kalamata Olive Bread
Makes 1 loaf

4	tablespoons butter
½	cup pureed cooked rice (see appendix)
1	cup buttermilk
4	eggs
1 ½ cups GF flour mixture for savory recipe (see appendix)	
1	teaspoon baking powder
¼	teaspoon sea salt
1	cup chopped kalamata olives
1	tablespoon chopped rosemary

Mix flour with the salt, baking powder and rosemary.

Mix the butter with the cooked rice and the buttermilk. Whisk the eggs and add to the butter mixture.

Add the flour mixture ½ cup at a time and mix for smooth dough.

Add the chopped olives and gently fold couple times to incorporate the olives.

Grease bread pan with olive oil and spoon the dough into the pan.

Bake in 400 degrees F oven for 1 hour. Remove from the oven and allow the bread to cool before slicing.

White Bread
Makes 1 loaf

This recipe is adapted from Steve Schmidt of Baltic, South Dakota.

1½   cup white rice flour
1   cup brown rice flour
½   cup potato starch
½   cup sweet sorghum flour
3   tablespoons sugar
2⅓   teaspoons xanthan gum
1   teaspoon salt
2½   teaspoons yeast
1   cup warm milk
⅛   cup corn oil
⅔   teaspoon vinegar
2   eggs

Mix the dry ingredients, except the yeast.

Mix the sugar with the yeast and warm milk. Allow the yeast to rise.

Whisk the eggs with the corn oil, vinegar and the yeast mixture.

Add the egg mixture to the dry mixture and mix gently. You should have sticky dough. Cover and allow the dough to rise for 45 minutes.

Grease a 9x3 loaf pan, then spoon the dough into the pan. Cover and allow the dough to rest for another 30 minutes.

Bake in a 375 degrees F oven for 45-60 minutes or until golden and knife inserted inside comes clean. Remove from the oven and allow the loaf to cool on rack. Remove from the pan and slice.

Sauces

Sweet Baking

Savory Baking

Main Dishes

Salads

Soups

Appetizers

Multigrain Bread
Makes 1 loaf

2 ½	cups GF savory flour mixture (see appendix)	2	cups warm milk
½	cup quinoa flakes	6	tablespoons butter melted and cooled
½	cup blue corn meal med. grind	4	tablespoons puree candied orange (see appendix)
½	teaspoon salt	½	cup sun flower seeds
1	tablespoon yeast	2	tablespoons melted butter
1	teaspoon sugar		

Mix the flour with the quinoa flakes, the blue corn meal, and the salt.

Mix the butter with the candied oranges.

Dissolve the sugar and the yeast in the warm milk and allow it to rest for 5 minutes, and then pour over the butter. Mix well.

Add the flour mixture into the liquid and mix into smooth dough.

Fold in the sun flower seeds.

Spoon the dough into 9 by 5-inch bread pan. Cover with a towel and allow the dough to rest for 30 minutes.

Bake the bread 350 degrees F oven for 40 minutes.

Remove from the oven and with sharp knife slash the loaf ½ inch deep along the long side of the loaf. Pour half of the butter in the slash and brush the top with the rest of the butter.

Return to the oven and bake for extra 5 minutes.

Remove from the oven and cool for 10 minutes and then turn onto rack and allow the bread to cool before slicing.

Sweet Potato Bread
Makes 2 loaves

1	cup baked and pureed sweet potatoes
1	cup boiled and puree rice (see appendix)
2	tablespoons pureed candied orange (see appendix)
¼	cup sugar
½	cup ghee
¼	cup almond milk
1	tablespoon yeast
2	eggs
3	cups GF flour mixture for sweet recipe (see appendix)
1	cup quinoa flakes
½	teaspoon salt
1	cup raisins

Mix the flour with the quinoa and salt.

Mix the yeast with 1 tablespoon sugar. Heat the almond milk until warm and pour over the yeast. Stir and allow the yeast to rise.

Mix the pureed sweet potato with the pureed rice, pureed candied orange, sugar and the ghee. Add the milk yeast mixture and mix gently. Don't over mix.

Whisk the eggs and add to the rice and milk mixture. Start to add the flour mixture to the egg mixture one cup a time. Add the raisins and mix gently into smooth dough. Spoon into 2 bread pans.

Bake in 395 degrees F oven for 1 hour. Remove from the oven and allow the bread to cool for 1 hour before slicing.

Sauces

Sweet Baking

Savory Baking

Main Dishes

Salads

Soups

Appetizers

Yam and Raisin Bread
Makes 2 loaves

½   cup pureed cooked rice (see appendix)
½   cup pureed candied oranges (see appendix)
2   baked small yams, peeled and pureed
½   cup sugar
4   tablespoons butter
2   cups GF flour mixture for sweet recipe (see appendix)
1   tablespoon baking powder
½   teaspoon salt
¼   cup raisins
3   eggs

Mix the flour with the baking powder and the salt.

Cream the butter with the sugar. Add the rice, the pureed orange and the yams, and cream into a smooth paste. Whisk the eggs and add to this mixture.

Add the flour and the raisins and gently fold into smooth dough.

Spoon into small bread pan. Bake in 400 degrees F oven for 1 hour. Remove from the oven and cool for couple hours before serving.

Sauces

Sweet Baking

Savory Baking

Main Dishes

Salads

Soups

Appetizers

Zucchini Raisins Bread
Makes 2 loaves

3	cups GF flour mixture for sweet recipe (see appendix)
1	teaspoon cinnamon
½	teaspoon freshly ground nutmeg
½	teaspoon ground cloves
1	teaspoon salt
1	teaspoon baking powder
1	teaspoon baking soda
6	tablespoons unsalted butter
1 ½	cups sugar
3	large eggs
¼	cup plain yogurt
2	tablespoons pureed candied orange or orange marmalade

Mix the flour with the cinnamon, the nutmeg, the cloves, the salt, the baking powder and the baking soda.

Cream the butter with the sugar, and then add the eggs and whisk thoroughly. Add the yogurt, the pureed candied oranges and the zucchini and mix.

Pour flour mixture over the egg batter and stir thoroughly.

Pour the batter to greased 8 ½ X 4 ½ in bread pan.

Bake in a 350 degrees F oven for one hour or until toothpick comes out clean. Cool for 30 minutes before slicing.

SWEET BAKING

Walnut Bread
Makes 1 loaf

2	cups GF flour mixture for sweet recipe (see appendix)
1	teaspoon salt
1	tablespoon baking powder
1	teaspoon baking soda
2	tablespoons cinnamon
1	large egg
½	cup pureed cooked rice (see appendix)
3	tablespoons ghee
½	cup brown sugar
1	cup chopped walnuts

Mix the flour with the salt, the baking powder, the baking soda and the cinnamon.

Mix the ghee with the sugar and the cooked rice. Whisk the egg and add to the ghee.

Pour flour mixture over the ghee batter and stir thoroughly. Fold in the walnuts.

Pour batter into the loaf pans, about 2/3 full.

Bake in a 395 degrees F oven for 35-45 minutes or until toothpick comes out clean.

Christmas Bread
Makes 1 loaf

½   cup pureed cooked rice (see appendix)
¼   cup butter
½   cup sugar
2   eggs
1   cup almond milk
3   Tablespoons orange juice
3   cups GF flour mixture for sweet recipe (see appendix)
¼   teaspoon salt
1   teaspoon baking powder
¼   cup chopped candied orange peels (see appendix)
¼   cup cranberries

Mix the flour with the salt and the baking powder.

Cream the butter with the sugar into smooth cream. Add the pureed cooked rice and mix well.

Whisk the eggs, and then add the almond milk and the orange juice and mix. Pour over the creamed sugar and mix.

Add the flour, ½ cup at time, to the liquid mixture until you have smooth little runny dough.

Fold the candied orange peels and the cranberries and spoon into loaf pan.

Bake in a 400 degrees F oven for 1 hour. Remove and allow to cool before slicing.

Sauces

Sweet Baking

Savory Baking

Main Dishes

Salads

Soups

Appetizers

Cinnamon Buns (1)
Makes 12 buns

3	cups GF flour mixture for sweet recipe (see appendix)	2	tablespoons pureed candied orange (see appendix)
½	salt	1	egg
1 ½	cups boiled and pureed rice (see appendix)	¼	cup Ghee
½	cup warm milk	½	cup sugar
1	tablespoon yeast	3	tablespoons cinnamon

Mix the flour with the salt.

Mix the yeast with 1 teaspoon sugar in the warm milk. Allow the mixture to rest for 10 minutes.

Mix the pureed candied orange with the pureed rice and the egg. Add the milk mixture and mix gently. Don't over mix.

Place the flour mixture in a blow. Add the milk rice mixture and mix into smooth dough.

Place wax paper on tables and grease with little of ghee. Place the dough over the wax paper and roll into ¼ inch thick 12 by 12 square.

Spread the ghee over the dough. Mix the sugar with the cinnamon and sprinkle over the ghee. Press gently into the dough.

Using the wax paper, slowly and carefully roll the dough into a tight log.

Turn the cylinder so the end edge is on the bottom.

Gently with the use of serrated knife cut the cylinder into 12 1-inch thick rolls.

Arrange the rolls in greased baking pan, cover and allow the rolls to rest for 1 hour.

Bake in 375 degrees F oven for 25 minutes or until the rolls are golden. Remove from the oven, cool slightly and serve.

Sauces

Sweet Baking

Savory Baking

Main Dishes

Salads

Soups

Appetizers

Cinnamon Buns (2)
Makes 12 buns

1	cup warm buttermilk		1	tablespoon yeast
5	tablespoons butter		½	teaspoon salt
2	eggs		2	tablespoons unsalted butter
2	tablespoons pureed cooked rice (see appendix)			at room temperature
2 ½	cup GF flour sweet (see appendix)		½	cup brown sugar
¼	cup sugar		2	tablespoons cinnamon

Melt the butter but do not boil. Add the buttermilk to the butter and mix. Whisk the eggs, and then add to the buttermilk. Set aside.

Mix the flour with the sugar, the yeast and the salt.

Add the flour mixture to the buttermilk mixture and gently fold until you added all the flour and you have sticky dough. Add the cooked rice and knead until you have smooth dough.

Dust your counter with little of GF flour. Place the dough on the counter and roll into 12-inch square. Mix the brown sugar with the cinnamon.

Spread the unsalted butter over the dough and sprinkle the brown sugar and cinnamon mixture. Press the cinnamon mixture gently into the dough.

Use metal spatula to loosen the dough from the counter. Roll the dough into a tight log. Moisten the end of the dough and gently push to seal.

Use serrated knife and cut the cylinder into 12 1-inch wide rolls. Arrange the buns on greased large baking pan.

Cover and allow the buns to rest and rise for 20 minutes.

Bake in 350 degrees F oven for 30 minutes.

Walnut Cinnamon Bread
Makes 1 loaf

1   **cinnamon bun (2) dough**
1   **cup coarsely chopped walnuts**
2   **tablespoons sugar**
1   **tablespoon cinnamon**
¼   **cup orange blossom water syrup (see appendix)**
2   **tablespoons orange liquor**

Mix the walnuts with the sugar and the cinnamon and spoon into the bottom of bundt cake pan.

Place the dough over the walnut mixture and tap gently to even the dough.

Cover the pan and allow the bread to rest at room temperature for 45 minutes.

Bake in 350 degrees F oven for 35 minutes.

Take the bread out of the oven. Mix the orange liquor with the syrup and drizzle over the hot bread. Allow the bread to cool before unmolding and slicing the bread.

Almond Cake
Serves 8-10

½ cup raisins soak for 1 hour in orange juice
2 cups GF sweet four mixture (see appendix)
½ cup almond flour
2 teaspoons baking powder
1 teaspoon sea salt
½ cup ghee
1 ½ cup sugar
1 cup pureed candied orange (see appendix)
3 eggs
1 cup almond milk

Whisk the eggs and add the almond milk and the candied oranges.

Mix the ghee with the sugar into smooth paste. Add to the milk mixture and mix well.

Mix the flours with the sea salt and the baking powder. Add the flour mixture, ½ cup a time, and mix well. Add the raisins and spoon into greased cake pan.

Bake in 395 degrees F oven for 1 hour.

Sauces

Sweet Baking

Savory Baking

Main Dishes

Salads

Soups

Appetizers

Almond Orange Cake
Serves 8

½   cup cold orange blossom water syrup
½   cup pureed candied oranges (see appendix)
4   eggs
½   cup Greek yogurt
½   cup sugar
3   cups almond flour
½   cup GF flour mixture for sweet recipe (see appendix)
½   teaspoon salt
½   teaspoon baking soda

Mix the syrup with the candied oranges and set aside.

Whisk the eggs and then add the yogurt and mix well.

Place the almond flour in heavy cast iron pan and slightly toast the almond flour for couple minutes stirring often. Remove the flour and cool and spoon into bowl. Add the GF flour, baking soda and the salt.

Pour the yogurt over the flour and mix well. Spoon the dough into 9 X 9-inch baking pan.

Bake in 395 degrees F oven for 30 minutes or until the cake is golden.

Pour the cold syrup over the hot cake. Cool for 30 minutes before serving.

Sauces

Sweet Baking

Savory Baking

Main Dishes

Salads

Soups

Appetizers

Orange Cream Cheese Cake
Makes 2 loaves

4	ounces cream cheese
½	cup butter
1 ½	cup sugar
2	eggs
½	cup pureed candied orange (see appendix)
2 ½	cups GF sweet four mixture (see appendix)
½	cup dry coconut flakes
½	teaspoon ground fennel seeds
1	teaspoon baking powder
½	teaspoon salt
½	cup milk
½	cup orange juice
1	teaspoon orange blossom water

Cream the cream cheese with the butter, the sugar and the candied pureed orange.

Whisk the eggs and add to the cream cheese mixture.

Mix the milk with the orange juice and the orange blossom water. Set aside.

Mix the flour with the coconut flakes, the fennel seeds, the baking powder and the salt.

Add 1/3 of the dry ingredient to the egg mixture and mix well. Add ½ of the milk mixture and mix well. Repeat until you used all the flour and the milk.

Grease 9 X 5-inch loaf pan. Spoon the dough into the pan and bake in 395 degrees F oven for 45-60 minutes. Remove from the oven and cool in the pan for 30 minutes. Take out the loaf and place it on a cooling rack.

Coconut Dream Cake
Makes 1 loaf

⅓   of the orange cream cheese cake dough
⅓   cup pureed candied orange (see appendix)
⅓   cup orange juice
½   cup coconut flakes

Grease small cake pan. Sprinkle with ¼ cup of the coconut flakes.

Gently mix the dough with the candied orange, the orange juice and the rest of the flakes.
Spoon this mixture into the prepared cake pan.

Bake in 395 degrees F oven for 45 minutes. Remove from the oven and cool for 1 hour
before flipping the cake and slicing.

Almond Sponge Cake
Serves 8

2   cups almonds flour
1   cup quinoa flour
1   cup ground almonds, toasted
1   tablespoon baking powder
2   tablespoon xanthan gum
1   cup sugar
6   tablespoons butter
3   eggs
½   cup orange marmalade
¼   cup orange juice
zest of one orange
2   tablespoons powdered sugar for garnish

Preheat oven to 350 degrees F.

Grease a bundt cake pan.

Mix both flours with the baking powder, the gum and the toasted almonds.

In a chilled bowl, mix the butter and the sugar until fluffy. Add the eggs one at a time. Stir in the flour mixture, orange marmalade, orange juice, and the orange zest. Spoon the mixture into the prepared baking pan.

Bake in the preheated oven for 40-50 minutes or until inserted knife comes out clean. Remove from the oven and allow to cool on a rack.

Remove the cake from the pan, place on a shallow serving platter and dust with the powdered sugar.

Sauces

Sweet Baking

Savory Baking

Main Dishes

Salads

Soups

Appetizers

Cinnamon Biscotti
Makes about 30 biscotti

2	cups GF sweet all purpose flour mixture (see appendix)	6	tablespoons unsalted butter, room temperature
3	teaspoons ground cinnamon	3	large eggs
1	teaspoon baking powder	½	cup orange juice
¼	teaspoon salt	1	teaspoon vanilla extract
1	cup sugar		

Preheat the oven to 325 degrees F.

Mix flour, 2 teaspoons cinnamon, baking powder and salt.

With an electric mixer, beat all the sugar—except for 2 tablespoons—and butter until fluffy.

Add 2 eggs and beat well. Mix in vanilla extract and orange juice.

Add the flour cinnamon mixture and mix well. Divide the dough in half.

Shape each half into nine-inch long log.

Transfer logs to parchment lined cookie sheet.

Beat remaining egg in a small bowl, brush logs with the egg wash.

Bake in the preheated oven for 40 minutes.

Remove from the oven and cool for 15 minutes. Maintain oven temperature.

Mix the rest of the sugar with the rest of the cinnamon.

Using serrated knife, cut log at thirty five degree angle into 1/2-inch thick slices.

Place the biscotti, cut side down, on a baking sheet.

Sprinkle cinnamon sugar mixture over each biscotti. Bake for 15 minutes. Remove from the oven and cool on a rack.

Sauces

Sweet Baking

Savory Baking

Main Dishes

Salads

Soups

Appetizers

Pistachio Biscotti
Makes 24 biscotti

1 ½ cup GF sweet flour mixture
(see appendix)
½ almond flour
4 tablespoons unsalted butter, softened
1 ½ cup pureed candied oranges
(see appendix)
1 cup packed brown sugar

1 egg
½ cup ground toasted almonds
1 teaspoon baking powder
1 teaspoon vanilla extract
½ teaspoon cinnamon
¼ teaspoon salt
1 cup shelled unsalted pistachios

In a food processor, beat the butter with the sugar until creamy.

Add orange puree and vanilla extract and mix more.

Add the egg and beat well.

Mix the flours with the baking powder, the cinnamon and the salt. Add the flour mixture to the egg mixture and beat thoroughly.

Move the dough into two parts and shape each part into 12 inch long logs.

Place both logs on a cookie sheet. Set them 3 inches apart.

Refrigerate for 2 hours.

Preheat the oven to 325 degrees F.

Bake for 35 minutes, or dry to touch.

Let cool for about 30 minutes, and then cut the logs on the diagonal into 1/2-inch thick slices.

Arrange the biscotti on the cookie sheet next to each other. Bake for 20 minutes.

Remove from the oven and cool on a rack or 1 hour.

The biscotti can be stored in a covered cookie tin for 1 week.

Chocolate Hazelnut Biscotti
Makes 24 biscotti

½   **cup butter, room temperature**
½   **cup sugar**
2   **tablespoons pureed candied oranges (see appendix)**
2   **tablespoons buttermilk**
1   **tablespoon vanilla**
⅓   **cup unsweetened cocoa powder**
1   **teaspoon baking powder**
1   **teaspoon baking soda**
½   **teaspoon salt**
2   **eggs**
1 ½ **cup GF flour mixture for sweet recipe (see appendix)**
½   **cup hazelnut flour**

Mix the cocoa powder with both flours, the baking powder, the baking soda and the salt.

Cream the butter with the sugar into smooth paste. Add the candied oranges, the buttermilk and the vanilla. Add the eggs and mix well.

Add the flour mixture into the egg mixture.

Divide the dough into 3 balls. Roll and form each ball into 2-inch thick log. Place each log on a cookie sheet.

Bake in 375 degrees F oven for 20 minutes. Take out of the oven and cool for 15 minutes. Turn the temperature to 350 degrees F.

Place the baked log at 45 degrees and cut ½ inch thick slices. Place the slices on another cookie sheet and bake for 7 minutes.

Chocolate Biscotti
Makes 24 biscotti

½   **cup unsalted butter**
½   **cup sugar**
2   **tablespoons pureed candied orange (see appendix)**
⅓   **cup unsweetened cocoa powder**
1   **teaspoon baking powder**
1   **teaspoon baking soda**
½   **teaspoon salt**
2   **eggs**
1 ½ **cup GF flour mixture for sweet recipe (see appendix)**
½   **cup hazelnut flour**
½   **cup semisweet chocolate chips**

Mix the cocoa powder with the baking soda, the baking powder and the salt.

Cream the butter with the sugar and the candied orange. Add the cocoa powder and beat for couple minutes.

Add the eggs and beat until well mixed.

Mix the all purpose flour and the hazelnut flour and then add to the egg mixture. Gently fold in the chocolate chips.

Divide the dough into 2 logs, wrap and chill for 1 hour.

Remove from the refrigerator and bake in 375 degrees F oven for 20 minutes. Remove from the oven and cool for 1 hour.

Place each log at 45 angle and cut ½-inch wide slices. Place the slices on cookie sheet and bake in 350 degrees F oven for 10 minutes. Remove and cool before serving.

Sauces

Sweet Baking

Savory Baking

Main Dishes

Salads

Soups

Appetizers

Date and Apricot Cookies
Makes 24 cookies

1 ½ cup GF flour mixture for sweet recipe (see appendix)
½   teaspoon ground anise seeds
⅛   teaspoon salt
¼   pureed cooked rice (see appendix)
1   tablespoon vegan butter
2   tablespoons sugar
2   cups pureed dates
1   cup pureed dried apricots
½   cup coarsely chopped toasted walnuts

Mix the dates with the apricots and the walnuts. Roll it into ½ inch thick 24 long cylinder.

In another bowl, mix the flour with the anise seeds and the salt. Make a hole in the middle and add the pureed rice and the vegan butter. Start to incorporate the flour into the pureed rice. When the flour is totally incorporated into the pureed rice, add couple teaspoon of cold water and knead into smooth dough. Cut the dough into 4 balls.

Place wax paper on a counter and spread each ball into 8 inch long and 4 inch wide rectangle. Place ¼ of the date apricot cylinder and, with the help of the wax paper, fold the dough over the date to cover the date and make thick roll. Place the date roll covered with wax paper on cookie sheet. Repeat until you finish the dough.

Chill the stuffed rolls for an hour. Remove from the refrigerator, remove the wax gently and cut each roll into 8 slices.

Place the cookies on cookie sheet and bake in 395 degrees F oven for 35 minutes.

Remove from the oven and cool.

Sauces

Sweet Baking

Savory Baking

Main Dishes

Salads

Soups

Appetizers

Pound Cake
Serves 8

2	cups GF flour mixture for sweet recipe (see appendix)
1	teaspoon sea salt
1	tablespoon baking powder
1	cup unsalted butter
2	cups sugar
4	large eggs
¼	cup orange juice
2	tablespoons pureed candied oranges (see appendix)
1	zest of one lemon
2	tablespoons cream cheese

Mix the flour with the salt and the baking powder.

Beat the butter for couple minutes. Add the sugar and beat until into smooth cream. Add the eggs, the orange juice, the lemon zest, the cream cheese and the candied oranges.

Add the flour mixture into the egg mixture ½ cup at time. Mix into smooth sticky dough.

Grease 9 X 5-inch loaf pan and pour the dough into the pan.

Bake in 325 degrees F oven for 45 minutes. Remove from the oven, cool before serving.

Carrot Cake
Makes 16 servings

1   **pound carrots, enough to make one and half cups after boiled and mashed**
2   **cups GF sweet flour mixture (see appendix)**
1 ½ **cups sugar**
2   **teaspoons baking powder**
1   **teaspoon baking soda**
1   **teaspoon cinnamon**
1   **teaspoon nutmeg**
1   **teaspoon cardamom**
½   **teaspoon salt**
1   **cup pureed candied orange (see appendix)**
4   **eggs**
1   **cup raisins**
½   **cup chopped walnuts**
4   **cloves**
4   **whole cardamom**

Preheat the oven to 395 degrees F.

In a heavy pot, cover the carrots, cloves and whole cardamom in water and boil until carrots are soft.

Drain the carrots; discard the cloves and the cardamom. Puree the carrots in a food processor.

In a large bowl, combine the pureed carrots with the rest of the ingredients except the nuts and the raisins.

Beat at low speed for 4 minutes and then stir in the nuts and the raisins.

Grease 13 X 9 inch pan.

Pour into the greased pan and bake for 45-60 minutes in the preheated oven or until toothpick inserted in center comes out clean. Remove from the oven and cool completely.

Sauces

Sweet Baking

Savory Baking

Main Dishes

Salads

Soups

Appetizers

Raisin Cornmeal Cookies
Makes 3 dozen cookies

1 ½ cups GF sweet flour mixture (see appendix)
1   cup yellow cornmeal
½   cup sugar
¾   cup dark raisins
2   eggs, room temperature
4   tablespoons unsalted butter
½   cup apricot butter
½   cup pureed candied orange (see appendix)
1   teaspoon ground anise seeds
2   teaspoons baking powder
dash of salt

Soak the raisins in hot water for 30 minutes, drain and toss with 1 tablespoon of the flour.

Beat the butter, sugar, apricot butter and orange puree until smooth paste.

Add the eggs, one at a time. Beat after each addition.

In a bowl, mix the flour, the cornmeal, the anise seeds, the baking powder and salt. Add the flour mixture to the egg-butter mixture and mix thoroughly. Add the raisins and mix.

Transfer the dough to a light floured surface. Divide the dough into two balls. Roll each ball into two inches thick log.

Slice the log at half-inch thick rounds.

Place cookies on a greased cookie sheets about 2 inches apart.

Bake in a 375 degrees F oven until lightly browned, about 20 minutes.

Remove from the oven and cool on a rack.

Basic Tart Dough
Makes 8 mini tarts or 2 9-inch tarts

2   **cups GF savory flour mixture (see appendix)**
½   **cup brown sugar**
1   **pinch of salt**
1½ **stick unsalted butter, room temperature**
2   **eggs**
1   **teaspoon vanilla extract**
zest of two lemons

Cream the butter and the sugar until pale and creamy. Add the eggs, the vanilla and the lemon zest and beat until well blended.

Scrape down the sides of the bowl. Add the flour and beat until the dough forms a sticky ball.

Shape the dough into a disk, and wrap well in plastic. Refrigerate for at least 1 hour.

Remove the dough from the refrigerator and place on a floured surface. Cut the dough into 8 pieces. Roll each piece into 5 inches round.

Gently place the round inside tart pan with a removable bottom. Press gently inside the bottom of the ring to form a nice mold. Place the tart pans on a cookie sheet and chill for 30 minutes.

Place the cookie sheet in the middle of a 375 degrees F oven and bake for 10 minutes for partially baked shells or 15 minutes for fully baked shells.

Remove from the oven and cool completely in the tart pan before unmolding.

Basic Vegan Chocolate Tart Dough
Makes 8 mini tarts or 2 9-inch tarts

1½ cups GF sweet flour mixture (see appendix)
½ cup unsweetened Dutch processed cocoa powder
½ teaspoon sea salt
¼ cup brown sugar
¼ cup pureed candied orange (see appendix)
½ cup coconut oil
¼ cup pureed cooked rice (see appendix)

Mix the flour with the cocoa powder and the salt.

Cream the sugar with the coconut oil, the candied orange and the pureed rice.

Scrap the side of the bowl, and then add the flour cocoa mixture and beat until the dough forms a sticky mass.

Shape the dough into a disk and wrap well in plastic and refrigerate for two hours.

Remove the dough from the refrigerator and place on a floured surface. Roll and flatten the dough into ⅛-inch thick round.

Gently place the round inside tart pan with a removable bottom. Press gently inside the bottom of the ring to form a nice mold. Place the tart pans on a cookie sheet and chill for 30 minutes.

Place the cookie sheet in the middle of a 375 degrees F oven and bake for 10 minutes for partially baked shells or fifteen minutes for fully baked shells.

Remove from the oven and cool completely in the tart pan before unmolding.

Sauces

Sweet Baking

Savory Baking

Main Dishes

Salads

Soups

Appetizers

Apricot and Pistachio Tarts

8   **partially baked tart shells**
2   **cups ricotta cheese**
1   **tablespoon sugar**
1   **10-ounce can apricot, drained and chopped**
2   **tablespoons finely ground pistachios**

Mix the ricotta with the sugar and the apricot.

Spoon the ricotta mixture inside the tarts.

Bake in a 375 degrees F oven for ten minutes. Remove from the oven and cool slightly.

Sprinkle with the pistachio and serve.

Figs and Chocolate Tarts

8   partially baked chocolate tart shells
1   cup sweetened coconut milk
2   cups chopped dried figs
1   cup unsweetened shredded coconut
½   teaspoon ground anise seeds

Toss figs with the shredded coconuts and the ground anise seeds.

Add the coconut milk over the figs mixture and mix well.

Place the tart shells on cookie sheet. Divide the fig mixture evenly among the tart shells.

Bake in a 350 degrees F oven for 20 minutes, or until the coconut is lightly toasted. Remove from the oven and allow tarts to cool 30 minutes before serving.

Sauces

Sweet Baking

Savory Baking

Main Dishes

Salads

Soups

Appetizers

Chocolate and Strawberry Tarts

8   **fully baked chocolate tarts**
2   **cups whipped cream**
8   **strawberries**
2   **tablespoons finely shaved sweet chocolate**

Place each tart on a white serving dish.

Spoon whipped cream inside each tart.

Place one strawberry, with its cap still on, upright on each tart.

Sprinkle the shaved chocolate over and around each tart and serve.

Nammoraa, Corn and Coconut Bars
Makes about 20 bars

2	tablespoons tahini (see appendix)
4	cups yellow corn meal
1	cup unsweetened shredded coconuts
1	cup sugar
½	cup melted butter
2	cups plain yogurt
1	teaspoon baking powder
½	teaspoon baking soda
4	cups sugar syrup

Mix corn meal, coconuts, sugar and butter.

Mix yogurt with the baking soda and the baking powder. Add the corn meal mixture and blend into smooth paste.

Grease 17 X 12 inches pan with tahini. Pour the mixture into the pan and smooth the top. Cut into 2-inches wide bars.

Bake in a 400 degrees F oven for 30 minutes, or until brown.

Pour the syrup on top and allow to cool before serving.

Sauces

Sweet Baking

Savory Baking

Main Dishes

Salads

Soups

Appetizers

Double Chocolate Scones
Makes 10 scones

1	cup soy flour	2	teaspoon baking powder
2	cups hazelnut flour	1	teaspoon baking soda
⅓	cup unsweetened cocoa powder	¼	teaspoon salt
½	cup packed brown sugar	1	egg yolk, beaten
½	cup olive oil	½	cup semisweet chocolate chips
⅓	cup orange preserve	1	teaspoon powdered sugar, optional
8	ounces non-fat plain yogurt		

Preheat oven to 350 degrees F.

In a large bowl stir together flour, cocoa powder, brown sugar, baking powder, baking soda and salt.

Add olive oil and mix until mixture resembles coarse crumbs.

Combine egg yolk, yogurt and orange preserve.

Add yogurt mixture into the dry ingredients. Mix well.

Add chocolate chips. Stir mixture until moistened.

On a lightly floured surface, gently knead dough until dough is nearly smooth.

Pat dough into a 9-inch circle; cut into 10 wedges.

Place wedges 1 inch apart on an ungreased baking sheets.

Bake for 30 minutes.

Remove from baking sheet; cool on wire rack for 5 minutes.

Dust top with powdered sugar. Serve warm.

Sauces

Sweet Baking

Savory Baking

Main Dishes

Salads

Soups

Appetizers

Sweet Potato Scones
Makes 10 scones

2	sweet potatoes baked, peeled and mashed
½	coconut oil
½	cup almond milk
1	tablespoon lemon juice
2	tablespoons pureed candied orange (see appendix)
3	cups GF sweet flour mixture
½	cup sugar
1½	teaspoon baking powder
1	teaspoon baking soda
¼	teaspoon salt
½	teaspoon anise seeds
½	teaspoon ground nutmeg
½	tablespoon olive oil

Mix the sweet potatoes with the coconut oil, the almond milk, the lemon juice and the candied oranges.

Mix the flour with the sugar, the baking powder, the baking soda, the salt, the anise seeds and the nutmeg.

Add the flour mixture into the sweet potato mixture ½ cup a time and mix, using spatula, into smooth dough.

Spoon 10 balls into cookie sheet. Grease the palms with olive oil and smooth each ball into 1 inch thick oval.

Bake in a 425 degrees F oven for 25 minutes.

Figs and Ginger Scones
Makes 8 scones

8   tablespoons chilled butter, cut into small pieces
1   cup chopped dried figs
2   tablespoons fig jam
1   teaspoon chopped candied ginger
¼   teaspoon lemon oil for cooking or lemon zest
1   cup buttermilk
2   cups GF sweet flour mixture (see appendix)
½   cup sugar
2   teaspoons baking powder
½   teaspoon baking soda
½   teaspoon salt
1   melted butter
1   tablespoon raw sugar

Mix the sweet flour with the sugar, the baking powder, the baking soda, and the salt.

Add the butter and mix into small crumbles. Add the buttermilk and the lemon oil. Mix well.

Place in large chilled ball and knead into smooth dough. Dust flat surface with little GF flour. Flatten into 1-inch thick 16 by 12-inch rectangle. Mix the figs with the fig jam and the candied ginger and then spoon and spread over the middle section of the rectangle. Gently, and with the help of metal spatula, fold into 16 X 4-inch rectangle. Press into thick log and press gently. Place the log on cookie sheet and chill for 1 hour. Take the log out and with sharp knife, cut into 8 triangle scones.

Place the scones on cookie sheet, brush with melted butter and sprinkle with the raw sugar. Bake in 425 degrees F oven for 15-20 minutes or the tops are lightly golden brown. Remove from the oven, cool for 15 minutes and enjoy.

Blueberry Scones
Makes 8 scones

5	tablespoons chilled butter, cut into small pieces
1	cup blueberries
¼	cup milk
¼	cup yogurt
2	cups GF sweet flour mixture (see appendix)
½	cup sugar
1	teaspoon baking soda
1	teaspoon baking powder
2	tablespoons pureed candied orange (see appendix)
¼	teaspoon salt

Mix the GF flour with the sugar, the baking soda, the baking powder and the salt. Add the butter and mix into coarse meal.

Mix the milk with the yogurt and the candied oranges. Add to the flour butter meal and with the help of spatula mix into smooth dough. Wrap and chill the dough for couple hours or overnight.

Dust flat surface with little GF flour. Roll and flatten the dough into 1-inch thick 16 by 12-inch rectangle. Spread the blueberry over the middle section of the rectangle. Gently, and with the help of metal spatula, fold into 16 X 4-inch rectangle. Press into thick log and press gently. Place the log on cookie sheet and chill for 1 hour. Take the log out and with sharp knife, cut into 8 triangle scones.

Place the scones on cookie sheet. Bake in 425 degrees F oven for 15-20 minutes or the tops are lightly golden brown. Remove from the oven, cool for 15 minutes and enjoy.

Sauces

Sweet Baking

Savory Baking

Main Dishes

Salads

Soups

Appetizers

Cinnamon Muffins
Makes 12 muffins

2   cups GF sweet flour mixture (see appendix)
½   cup sugar
½   cup brown sugar
1   tablespoon cinnamon
½   teaspoon baking soda
1   tablespoon baking powder
¼   teaspoon salt
1½   cup vanilla yogurt
2   eggs
8   tablespoons melted ghee

Mix the flour with the sugar, the brown sugar, the cinnamon, the baking soda, baking powder and the salt.

Whisk the eggs and add the yogurt and the ghee and mix well. Add the flour mixture into the yogurt mixture and fold, using spatula, into smooth batter.

Grease 12-cup muffin tin and spoon the batter evenly into the muffin cups.

Bake in 375 degrees F oven and bake for 25 minutes or until golden brown.

Remove the muffin from the oven and allow them to cool for 15 minutes before serving.

Sweet Potato Cookies
Makes 14 cookies

1   medium yam, baked
4   ounces raspberry jam
½   cup soy flour
1   teaspoon baking powder
¼   teaspoon cardamom
½   cup raisins
¼   cup sugar
2   eggs
1   tablespoon olive oil
zest of one lemon

Peel the baked yam and mash it. You should have about 3/4 cup of mashed yam.

Whisk the eggs with the sugar, the olive oil and the lemon zest. Add the yam and mix well.

Mix the dry ingredients and add to the yam mixture. Mix well.

Fold in the raisins.

Drop about tablespoon of dough onto a cookie sheet.

Bake in a 375 degrees F oven for 30 minutes.

Sauces

Sweet Baking

Savory Baking

Main Dishes

Salads

Soups

Appetizers

Coffee Raspberry Brownies
Makes 24 brownies

1   stick unsalted butter, room temperature
4   ounces coarsely chopped bitter chocolate
2   large eggs
1   cup sugar
¼   cup orange marmalade
¼   cup raspberry preserves
1   cup hazelnut flour
½   teaspoon baking powder
¼   teaspoon salt
1   cup chocolate covered espresso beans, coarsely ground

Grease and lightly flour a 9-inch square baking pan.

In a small heavy saucepan melt butter, add the chocolate and melt over low heat. Whisk to have smooth paste. Remove from the heat.

Whisk the eggs and the sugar. Add the marmalade and the raspberry jam. Whisk well. Add the melted chocolate.

Mix the flour with the baking powder, the salt and the chocolate espresso beans. Add flour mixture into the chocolate batter and beat well.

Spread the batter evenly in pan and bake in the middle of a 350 degrees F oven for 30 minutes, or until a tester comes out with crumbs adhering to it.

Cool brownies completely in pan on a rack before cutting into 24 squares.

Sauces

Sweet Baking

Savory Baking

Main Dishes

Salads

Soups

Appetizers

Chocolate Chunk Cookies
Makes 20 cookies

8   ounces semisweet chocolate squares
⅓   cup firmly packed brown sugar
2   tablespoons unsalted butter
1   egg
1   tablespoon vanilla extract
1   cup GF sweet flour mixture (see appendix)
¼   teaspoon baking powder
½   teaspoon salt
1   cup chopped toasted hazelnuts

Preheat oven to 350 degrees F.

Coarsely chop half of the chocolate squares into small chunks. Set aside.

Melt the remaining chocolate squares by placing them in metal bowl and then place the bowl over boiling water. Stir until the whole chocolate is melted.

Add the sugar, butter, eggs and vanilla extract to the melted chocolate and blend well.

Mix the flours with the baking powder and salt. Stir the flour mixture in to the egg-chocolate mixture. Mix well.

Stir in the chocolate chunks and the hazelnuts.

Spoon 1 tablespoon of the dough, 2 inches apart, onto an ungreased cookie sheet.

Bake for 12 minutes. Remove from the oven and cool for 10 minutes. Remove cookies from the cookie sheet and cool completely on a rack before serving.

Fudge Brownies with Chocolate Chips
Makes 24 brownies

1   cup soy flour
1   cup orange marmalade
4   ounces lite silken tofu, pureed
4   ounces unsweetened chocolate, chopped
3   eggs
½   cup sugar
¼   cup olive oil
2   teaspoon vanilla extract
½   cup semisweet chocolate chips
1   tablespoons powdered sugar

Grease 13 X 9 X 2 inch metal baking pan.

Preheat oven to 350 degrees F.

Place olive oil and chopped chocolate in a small metal bowl. Place the bowl on top of boiling water, stir until chocolate is melted and mixture is smooth. Remove from the heat.

In a large bowl, whisk eggs and sugar until pale yellow, about 3 minutes.

Gradually whisk in the warm chocolate mixture.

Whisk in orange marmalade, tofu and vanilla extract.

Mix in the flour, then chocolate chips.

Pour batter into greased baking pan.

Bake brownies for 25 minutes. Knife inserted in center should come out with moist crumbs attached.

Cool brownies completely in the pan on a rack.

Cut into squares. Sift powdered sugar on top.

Qatayif: Stuffed Thin Pancakes
Makes 12 qatayif

2	cups GF sweet flour mixture (see appendix)
1	cup pureed candied orange (see appendix)
2	tablespoons corn oil
½	cup sugar
½	teaspoon salt
1	tablespoon yeast
½	cup almond milk

Warm the almond milk, add the sugar and stir to dissolve. Add the yeast and stir. Add the candied oranges and the corn oil and whisk.

Add the flour and the salt and blend all well. Let the dough rise for 30 minutes.

Heat pancake pan and spoon ¼ cup of the dough over and cook until the bubbles at edge of the thin pancake start to dry, don't turn. Remove, with help of spatula, and place, cooked side down, on tray lined with kitchen towel.

Cool the qatayif and stuff.

Sauces

Sweet Baking

Savory Baking

Main Dishes

Salads

Soups

Appetizers

Walnut and sugar Qatayif
Makes 6 servings

12	freshly made qatayif
1	cup ground walnuts
½	cup sugar
1	tablespoon cinnamon
1	cup orange blossom water syrup (see appendix)

Mix the walnuts with the sugar and the cinnamon. Gently hold each qatayif , uncooked side up, and spoon 1 tablespoon of the walnut mixture into the qatayif and fold to half moon. Press the edges gently to seal. Place the stuffed qatayif on a cookie sheet and bake in 350 degrees F oven until golden or about 10 minutes.

Remove from the oven and drizzle with the syrup. Serve hot or cold.

Milk and Orange Pudding with Pistachio
Serves 4

4	cups 2% fat milk
1½	cups orange juice
1	cup sugar
5	tablespoons cornstarch
2	tablespoons orange blossom water (see appendix) or vanilla extract
½	cup crushed unsalted pistachios

Milk Pudding:

Dissolve 3 tablespoons of cornstarch and half of the sugar in the milk.

Heat the milk and simmer over medium-low heat, stirring constantly with a wooden spoon. When you feel resistance to the spoon and the mixture coats the spoon, turn off the heat. Stir 1 tablespoon of orange blossom water into the milk, then pour the pudding in 4 sundae dishes. Leave at least 1-inch from the top to make room for the orange pudding.

Let the milk pudding cool for an hour before adding the orange pudding.

Orange Pudding:

Dissolve the rest of the sugar and the rest of the cornstarch into the orange juice.

Heat the orange mixture and simmer over medium heat, stirring constantly with a wooden spoon. When the mixture coats the spoon, stir in one tablespoon of the orange blossom water and turn off the heat. Allow the orange pudding to cool for 10 minutes.

Slowly, pour a half-inch layer of orange pudding on top of the milk pudding.

Chill overnight. Sprinkle with the pistachios and serve cold.

Sauces

Sweet Baking

Savory Baking

Main Dishes

Salads

Soups

Appetizers

Bread Pudding
Serves 6-8

4	cups evaporated skim milk
2	cups Eggbeaters
½	cup sugar
½	cup orange marmalade
1	tablespoon vanilla extract
1	cup raisins
6	slices white sandwich bread (see recipe), remove crust and cut into 1-inch cubes

zest of one lemon

In a large bowl, whisk the milk, sugar and orange marmalade. Add the Eggbeaters, lemon zest and the vanilla extract.

Add the bread and raisins to the milk mixture, cover and refrigerate for one hour.

Pour the milk and bread mixture into 9 x 14 baking pan.

Bake in a 350 degrees F oven for one hour.

Remove from the oven. Allow the pudding to cool slightly, then serve.

Fig and Date Loaf
Serves 10

½   pound dried figs
½   pound pitted dates
1   cup coarsely chopped walnuts
2   tablespoons honey
½   teaspoon ground cloves
½   teaspoon ground cardamom
2   tablespoons powdered sugar
1   tablespoon ground pistachios

In a food processor, combine the figs with the dates and walnuts. Puree into a coarse mixture.

Add the honey, cloves and cardamom and process into a smooth mixture.

Spoon the mixture onto wax paper and shape into 3 inch thick cylinders.

Chill for a couple of hours.

When ready to serve: remove the wax paper, cut into 1-inch thick slices, then sprinkle with the powdered sugar and the pistachios.

Sauces

Sweet Baking

Savory Baking

Main Dishes

Salads

Soups

Appetizers

Poached Pears
Serves 8

4   Bosc pears, peeled, cut in half lengthwise
2   cups dry red wine
1   cup sugar
1   cup cranberry juice
½   cup dried cranberries
zest of one lemon

In a large stainless steel saucepan, combine all the ingredients, except the pears. Bring to a boil.

Reduce heat. Place the pears cut side down in the pan and simmer for 20 minutes.

Gently remove the pears and continue to simmer the wine sauce until it reduces to half its volume.

Place the pears cut side down on a white serving platter. Pour the wine sauce over and around the pears. Chill for a couple of hours before serving.

Almond Cookies
Makes 3 dozen

½ cup almond flour
1½ cup GF sweet flour mixture (see appendix)
6 ounces lite tofu
3 large eggs

2 tablespoons orange blossom water
2 cup almonds
1 teaspoon cardamom
¼ teaspoon salt

Preheat oven to 400 degrees F.

Butter and lightly dust with flour a 13 x 9 x 2 metal baking pan.

Mix flours, cardamom and salt in a bowl.

In a food processor, mix sugar, tofu, eggs and orange blossom water until blended well.

Add half of the flour mixture and blend well until mixed. Add the rest of the flour mixture and blend well.

Spoon the batter into a bowl. Stir in the almonds.

Spoon the batter into the greased baking pan.

Spray your palm with canola oil, and then with the palm smooth the top of the batter.

Bake for 20 minutes.

Cool for 10 minutes. Turn the pastry onto a rack and cool for 1 hour.

Place the pastry on a board and cut crosswise into ½-inch wide strips.

Cut each strip diagonally into 3 pieces.

Arrange cookies, cut side down, on baking sheets.

Bake until cookies are golden brown, about 10 minutes.

Transfer the cookies to a rack and cool for a couple of hours.

Sauces

Sweet Baking

Savory Baking

Main Dishes

Salads

Soups

Appetizers

Sesame Walnut Bars

Makes 24 bars

2½ cups GF sweet flour mixture (see appendix)
1   cup quinoa flour
1   cup packed brown sugar
1   teaspoon baking soda
¼   teaspoon salt
¾   cup unsalted butter
2   cups toasted sesame seeds in a 350 degrees F oven for 8 minutes
1   cup toasted hazelnuts
½   cup toasted walnuts
2   cups sugar
1   cup water
1   tablespoon lemon juice

Combine flour with the brown sugar, baking soda, salt and butter. Stir until all ingredients are moistened.

Press mixture into bottom of an ungreased 13 x 9 baking pan.

Bake in a 350 degrees F oven for 15 minutes. Remove from the oven and allow to cool completely.

In a heavy pot, bring water, sugar and lemon juice into a boil. Cook over medium heat until it becomes thick and sticky. Remove from heat, stir in the nuts and sesame seeds and spread over the baked crust.

Cool completely, then cut into 2-inch squares.

Apricot Squares
Makes 24

3	cups GF sweet flour mixture (see appendix)	1½	cups finely chopped dried apricots
½	cup hazelnut flour	2	cups light brown sugar
¾	cup unsalted butter	4	large eggs
4	tablespoons sugar	2	tablespoons vanilla extract
1	tablespoon orange blossom water, optional	¼	teaspoon salt
		¼	cup orange marmalade
		2	cups coarsely chopped toasted walnuts

To Make The Crust:

Mix 2 ½ cups of the GF flour with the hazelnut flour and sugar.

Add the butter and orange blossom water and gently mix until butter and flours are well mixed.

Press the dough into 16 x 9 baking pan.

Bake in a 350 degrees F oven for 10 minutes. Remove from the oven and cool for 10 minutes.

To Make The Squares:

Mix the rest of the GF sweet flour with the brown sugar, salt and apricots.

Whisk the eggs with the orange marmalade and the vanilla extract. Add the flour mixture and mix well. Pour this mixture over the baked crust.

Spread the toasted walnuts on top of the batter and press gently with a spatula into the batter.

Bake in a 350 degrees F oven for 35 minutes.

Remove from the oven and cool for a couple of hours before cutting.

Cut into 2-inch squares and serve.

Sauces

Sweet Baking

Savory Baking

Main Dishes

Salads

Soups

Appetizers

Date Bars
Makes 12 bars

½ cup unsalted butter
1½ cups white sorghum flour
2 tablespoons white sugar
1 teaspoon ground cardamom
1½ cups brown sugar
1 cup chopped walnuts
8 ounces chopped dates

3 eggs
3 tablespoons GF sweet flour mixture (see appendix)
½ teaspoon baking soda
1 tablespoon vanilla extract
¼ teaspoon salt

To Make The Crust:

Mix the white sorghum flour with the sugar and the cardamom. Add the butter and blend until you have coarse dough.

Press the dough firmly into the bottom of a 9-inch square cake pan.

Bake the dough in a 350 degrees F oven for 10 minutes. Remove from the oven and allow to cool for 15 minutes.

To Make The Bars:

Mix the brown sugar with the chopped walnuts, chopped dates, the GF flour, baking soda and salt.

Whisk the eggs and vanilla extract, and then add to the date mixture. Mix until well blended.

Pour the date batter over the baked crust. Tap the baking pan gently.

Bake in a 375 degrees F oven for 35 minutes.

Remove from the oven, place on a rack and allow it to cool for a couple hours.

Refrigerate for 30 minutes. Cut into 2-inch squares.

Maamoul: Walnut-Stuffed Cookies
Makes 30 cookies

3	cups walnuts		3	cups unsalted butter
1	cup sugar		1	teaspoon salt
2	tablespoons orange blossom water		1	teaspoon yeast
4	cups yellow cornmeal		¾	cup warm milk
2	cups white sweet sorghum flour		½	cup powdered sugar

To Make The Stuffing:

Place the walnuts, sugar and orange blossom water in a food processor and grind until it is a fine mixture. Spoon into a bowl and set aside.

To Make The Maamoul Dough:

Dissolve the yeast in the warm milk. Allow to set for a couple of minutes.

In a chilled bowl, mix both flours with the butter and the yeast mixture. Add more milk if the dough is dry.

To Make The Maamoul:

Divide the dough into walnut size balls. Smooth the balls round with the palm of your hand. With the forefinger, make a hole in dough and shape into a small cup like shape.

Spoon about a teaspoon of the filling into the cup and gently close the opening with your fingers. Place the closed side on a cookie sheet and gently flatten the bottom. You should have a dome shaped cookie. Decorate with the tip of a fork. Repeat these steps until you stuff and shape all the balls.

Bake in a 300 degrees F oven for 40 minutes, or until golden on the bottom of the cookies.

Remove from the oven, allow the cookies to cool for 1 hour, then dust with powdered sugar.

203

Rice Almond Pudding
Serves 8

½   cup slivered almonds
½   cup coarsely chopped walnuts
½   cup pistachios
½   cup short grain rice
5   cups almond milk
¼   cup rice flour
½   cup raisins
½   cup sugar
2   tablespoons orange blossom water (see appendix)
1   teaspoon crushed caraway seeds
½   teaspoon cinnamon
½   ground anise seeds

Place the almonds, walnuts and pistachios in a bowl and cover with cold water. Allow the nuts to soak in water for at least 2 hours before using them.

In a large heavy pot, cook the short grain rice in 1½ cups of water until the rice is soft, but not mushy.

Add the milk, sugar and rice flour to the cooked rice. Stir and cook over medium-low heat for 5 minutes.

Add the cinnamon, caraway seeds, ground anise seeds and raisins. Stir and bring the mixture to a simmer, stirring continuously, until thickened.

Pour the milk mixture into 8 custard cups. Cool for 15 minutes, then refrigerate for a couple of hours or overnight.

When ready to serve, drain the mixed nuts. Sprinkle the top of the pudding with the nuts and serve.

Sauces

Sweet Baking

Savory Baking

Main Dishes

Salads

Soups

Appetizers

SAUCES

Basic Tomato Sauce
Makes 3 cups

¼   **cup olive oil**
8   **cloves garlic, mashed**
8   **ounces can tomato paste**
2   **tablespoon chopped fresh basil or ½ teaspoon dry basil**
salt and pepper to taste

Heat the olive oil and sear the garlic for few seconds, make sure not to burn the garlic. Remove from the heat and add the tomato paste. Stir to blend well.

Add 3 cups of water, dry basil if you are using, salt and pepper. Mix until the tomato paste is dissolved and then place on the stove again. Bring to a boil. Cover and cook over medium-low heat for 10 minutes.

Turn off the heat and add the fresh basil.

Sauces

Sweet Baking

Savory Baking

Main Dishes

Salads

Soups

Appetizers

Tahini Sauce
Makes 2 cups

4	cloves garlic, mashed
1	teaspoon ground cumin
½	cup fresh squeeze lemon juice
½	cup water
¼	cup tahini
salt to taste	

In chilled bowl, mix all the ingredients together into smooth paste. Add little water if the sauce is thick.

Tahini and Pomegranate Sauce
Makes 2 cups

6   **cloves garlic, mashed**
1   **teaspoon ground cumin**
½   **teaspoon chili paste or ¼ teaspoon cayenne pepper**
½   **cup pomegranate molasses**
½   **cup tahini paste**
½   **cup lemon juice**
1   **cup water**
salt to taste

Mix the garlic with the cumin and the chili paste.

Add the rest of the ingredients and whisk into smooth paste.

Sauces

Sweet Baking

Savory Baking

Main Dishes

Salads

Soups

Appetizers

Spicy Walnut Sauce
Makes 2 cups

1	medium onion, finely chopped
4	cloves garlic, mashed
¼	cup olive oil
½	teaspoon cumin
½	teaspoon coriander
½	cup walnut, finely crushed
2	tablespoons chili paste or harissa
½	teaspoon cayenne pepper
¼	cup finely chopped cilantro
4	tablespoons pomegranate molasses
½	teaspoon tomato paste
½	cup lemon juice
1	cup water

salt to taste

Heat the olive oil and sauté the chopped onion until transparent. Add the garlic and the walnuts, and sauté for 5 minutes.

Add the cumin, the coriander, the chili paste, the cayenne pepper, the cilantro and sauté for extra couple minutes.

Add the pomegranate molasses, the tomato paste, the lemon juice, the salt and the water. Stir and bring to a boil. Cover and cook over very low heat for 5 minutes, stirring often.

Garlic and Lemon Sauce
Makes 1 cup

10   **cloves garlic, mashed**
1   **teaspoon sea salt**
2   **teaspoons finely chopped fresh rosemary**
1   **cup olive oil**
zest of two lemons

Place the garlic, the salt, the rosemary in a small food processor or blender. Puree until the garlic is coarsely crushed.

Continue to process while adding the olive oil drop by drop, you have to be very patient for great texture, continue until you have smooth light yellow paste.

Spoon into serving bowl, add the lemon zest and mix gently.

Sauces

Sweet Baking

Savory Baking

Main Dishes

Salads

Soups

Appetizers

ABOUT THE AUTHOR

A renowned chef, Sanaa Abourezk owns and operates a popular Middle East Restaurant in Sioux Falls, South Dakota. She earned a Bachelor of Science degree in Agricultural Engineering and a Masters degree in Nutrition from Cal Poly University in Pomona, California.

She attended a cooking school in Florence, Italy, and the Cordon Bleu Baking School in Paris, France.

She has worked as a nutrition adviser for the South Dakota Department of Health, where she advised clients on nutrition, cooking and healthy eating.

A talented creator of healthy and delicious recipes, she has published two cookbooks, *Secrets of Healthy Middle Eastern Cuisine*, and *Oh Boy, I Can't Believe It's Soy!*, both of which are best sellers.

Sanaa developed *Gluten Free Vegetarian Mediterranean Recipes* because of the many people who have told her of their suffering from celiac disease, which has severely hampered their enjoyment of food. This book is the result of long hours of research and recipe testing, and the author hopes that the recipes presented here allow more people with gluten sensitivities to enjoy these delicious dishes.

Sanaa blogs weekly at sanaacooks.com, posting recipes, cooking tips, and answering questions. Feel free to connect with her there and she will be happy to answer any questions you might have about her recipes or about cooking in general. Sanaa is continually creating new recipes, so be sure to check the blog at sanaacooks.com.

APPENDIX

Boiled rice: Place one cup of short grain rice and three cups of water in a pot and bring it to a boil. Turn the heat down and stir rice until it is overcooked and sticky. I use this as glue agent to hold the dough and make the bread moist.

Candied oranges: Cut the whole orange with the skin into 8 pieces and boil in hot water for 5 minutes. Drain and set aside. Mix 4 cups of water with 2 cups of sugar, place on the stove and bring to a boil. Drop the boiled orange in this syrup and cook over medium-low heat until the orange is transparent and the syrup is thicken, about 2 hours. Cool and then puree orange and syrup and spoon into sterilized jar. Refrigerate and use this in baking sweet.

Harissa: North African hot red pepper paste. Harissa is available in Middle Eastern and North African groceries.

Orange blossom water: It is a flavoring ingredient. You can use vanilla extract instead.

Pomegranate molasses: Concentrated syrup distilled from pomegranate juice, available in Middle Eastern groceries.

Savory gluten free flour mixture: 1 pound potato flour, 1 pound sweet white sorghum flour, 1 pound potato starch and 1 pound tapioca flour, 1 pound brown rice flour. Mix together and store in tight container.

Sweet gluten free flour mixture: 1 pound tapioca flour, 1 pound coconut flour, 1 pound sweet white sorghum flour and 1 pound potato flour. Mix together and store in tight container.

Tahini: Sesame seed paste.

INDEX OF RECIPES

Made in United States
Orlando, FL
08 January 2022